Emotional Intelligence 2.0

Master Your Emotions and Boost Your EQ - Increase Social Skills and Analyze People Better + Improve Self-Confidence and Your Nonverbal Communications.

Ferdinand Macy

TABLE OF CONTENTS

INTRODUCTION

Emotional intelligence is the ability to understand and regulate the emotions of yourself and others, and exists upon a large spectrum, in which some people are more or less emotionally intelligent than others.

While you may not have been blessed with a natural affinity for emotional intelligence as some people happen to be, however, you are not out of luck. Emotional intelligence is a skillset, and like other skillsets, even those without a natural tendency toward success in that skill can work their ways to higher levels of success. It is absolutely possible to teach yourself how to become emotionally intelligent, and this book is here to show you how today.

Within this book, you will find yourself introduced to emotional intelligence—learning the concept is the first step to improving upon your own innate abilities.

You will learn about the difference between an emotional intelligence quotient and intelligence quotient and why employers everywhere prefer EQ over IQ. You will learn about the various models of emotional intelligence, focusing on the ability model, the trait model, and the mixed model.

You will gain a functional understanding of the function of the brain, ranging from understanding the major parts of the brain, how the brain communicates through synapses, a look at neurotransmitters, and a glimpse at the parts of the brain that are particularly relevant to emotions and emotional regulation.

With that foundation of knowledge, you will begin to delve into truly understanding emotional intelligence as a concept. You will look at the pillars of emotional intelligence, understanding both personal and social competencies, as well as the various skillsets within each.

You will learn about persuasion and self-discipline, focusing on why each of them is important to being an emotionally intelligent individual. You will learn how to read people's verbal and nonverbal cues, an essential skill that is absolutely necessary to understand those around you.

You will learn how to reprogram your mind and focus on positive thinking, as when you are able to keep your thoughts positive, you are in a better frame of mind to really understand and influence those around you in a constructive manner.

Lastly, you will be provided with 15 different tips to improve your self-awareness, self-management, social awareness, and relationship management.

With the information provided in this book, you will be given all of the tools necessary to improve your own emotional intelligence.

You will be able to make yourself more capable of developing relationships with others and managing those relationships. In following the steps dictated within this book, you will likely see drastic improvements in your own relationships of all kinds—you will likely find yourself to be a better partner, friend, worker, and leader simply because you have worked on your own abilities.

With that said, you are now ready to begin your own journey toward becoming a more emotionally intelligent individual.

WHAT IS EMOTIONAL INTELLIGENCE?

Emotional intelligence, simply defined, is the ability to know, understand, control, use, and express personal emotions in order to be able to maintain relationships with other people and to do so empathetically and judiciously. It is the ability to know that actions are driven by emotions and that those emotions in other people can be used to better one's own position. People are affected by emotions, both negatively and positively, and people can learn how to manage their emotions.

Being able to manage one's emotions is important during times of stress and change when dealing with failure and setbacks when embroiled in challenging relationships, when receiving or giving feedback, or when personal resources are limited, and creativity must be used in order to survive and succeed. Emotional intelligence consists of being able to use these three skills: It is the ability to identify and understand one's own personal emotions; the knowledge to be able to use those emotions when problem-solving or brainstorming, and; the internal power to use personal emotions and the emotions of others whenever needed.

This does not necessarily mean that an emotionally intelligent woman is totally devoid of emotion. Rather it is the ability to manage and identify emotions. An emotionally intelligent woman is quite conscious of her own emotions, even the negative ones. And she is able to sense feeling in another person and has the power to use their emotions to gain her goal. This begins with self-awareness.

Personal self-awareness is the cornerstone of growth and success in one's personal life and the professional world. It is impossible to be emotionally intelligent without first being aware of what drives us emotionally. You must be able to see and understand your own emotions and accept them for what they are. You must realize that you alone have the power to control your emotions. When you begin to analyze your feelings and thoughts, and understand them better, you will begin to be able to have control over them instead of the other way around. You will be able to rule your emotions.

It is definitely not necessary to immediately react to every emotion and every event. You have the ability to choose which stimuli will cause you to act and which ones you will ignore. But to be able to do this, you must first admit that you have emotions and that those emotions are really good useful things. Once you begin to choose exactly how you will and will not respond, you begin to have control over your personal emotions. When your emotions rule you, then you are a prisoner of your own thoughts, and you will never have the freedom you deserve.

THE WILLPOWER INSTINCT: WHAT IT IS AND HOW IT WORKS

To understand what the willpower instinct is, you first have to understand the terms that make up the concept. The first term here is the word "will." "Will" refers to the ability to make conscious choices. You have heard of terms such as "free will." In many religious traditions, it's believed that free will is the one thing that makes human beings special or better than all other life forms; they have the ability to choose what to do. Your "will" is linked to your desires, and therefore, to the idea of success and self-determination.

The term "willpower" has lots of different definitions, but the simplest one is that: it's the motivation to exercise your will. We all have certain "wills" (they could be desires such as success, wealth, health, respect, etc.). additionally, we all have a general understanding of what we need to do to realize those wills or desires (for example, you know that you have to work out, eat nutritious foods and avoid harmful substances in order to be healthy). To move from having desires to realizing them, you need to have willpower. It's what will propel you from a dreamer to an achiever.

So, to put it simply, having a will means knowing what you want. Having willpower means that you have what it takes to get what you want. With the right amount of willpower, you can accomplish most of the goals that you have set for yourself. It could be something small (e.g., cleaning your room) or it could be something complex (e.g., earning your degree). Psychologists have found that willpower is better than intelligence when it comes to predicting success.

We all could benefit from having an unlimited supply of willpower. However, the fact is that we have a limited amount of willpower. Psychologists have found that willpower is like a battery; the more we use it, the more it gets depleted. For instance, studies done on college campuses show that when students are preparing for their exams, and they exert their willpower towards remembering the concepts and formulas, they tend to have less control over other aspects of their lives. For example, they tend to be more emotional, their personal hygiene declines, and they are more likely to smoke.

It seems that willpower is a "pooled resource." The willpower you exercise in all areas of your life comes from one place. That means that if you direct your willpower towards eating healthy, you may have less willpower to channel towards controlling you're spending.

Having willpower instinct is about understanding what you need to do to control your 'willpower exhaustion". You exert willpower in almost all areas of your life. This means that you have relatively high levels of willpower when you wake up in the morning, and it slowly gets depleted as the day progresses.

So, to manage the rate at which your willpower gets depleted, you first have to get a good night's sleep; this way, you will recharge your willpower and have enough supply to take you through the next day.

UNDERSTANDING YOUR THOUGHTS

Your thoughts can both create emotions, and be influenced by the emotions that you are already experiencing within your body. If you really want to learn how to have a stronger sense of emotional intelligence, you need to learn how your thoughts truly play into your emotional experience and what you can do about it. Learning how to navigate your thoughts purposefully will help you refrain from letting your thoughts get away from you and stimulate the production of more unwanted emotions, which can ultimately lead to you feeling like a powerless victim of your mind.

How Thoughts Create Emotions

The way that thoughts create emotions is best explained by cognitive behavioral therapy theory, as this theory provides a concise example of how your thoughts shape your experience and your feelings. Your thoughts are ultimately responsible for perceiving the world around you and creating a story in your mind to tell you what is going on. This story then becomes your reality as it is responsible for telling you what to focus on and what to pay the most attention to.

Typically, the thoughts that create your perception of your present surroundings and that create your perception of reality happen on a subconscious level. Sometimes, particularly when your subconscious mind identifies something that stimulates great emotion, this level of perception comes into your conscious awareness. Alternatively, if you tend to be highly present and in tune with your surroundings you might find yourself consciously thinking about your surroundings on a regular basis, too.

Once your subconscious thoughts have begun to stimulate the production of feelings, then your conscious thoughts start to reflect the feelings that are being produced. Through this, you find yourself thinking along the lines of whatever your emotions are. For example, you might think "I'm so angry," "This is not fair," or "I am really sad right now." At that point, your conscious thoughts are being shaped by the emotions that were triggered by your subconscious perception.

So, to summarize: your subconscious thoughts tend to perceive the world around you and create your reality. Sometimes, your conscious thoughts will be involved in this process too if you are feeling a particularly heightened emotion or if you are practicing being present. After your thoughts have created (what they believe to be) an accurate representation of your reality, you begin to experience emotions in response to that perceived reality. Through that, your emotions then begin to shape your experiences, including your thoughts and your continued perception of your reality based on the initial findings and emotional follow-up.

Learning to Manage Your Limiting Beliefs and Misleading Thoughts

In understanding that your thoughts shape your emotions in a big way, it is important to understand also that not every single thought you have is accurate. In other words, what you think to be true about your reality and what is actually true about your reality are not the same thing. As a result, much of what you think may be filled with limiting beliefs or misleading thoughts that are preventing you from being able to effectively think in a way that produces healthy and productive emotions in your life.

Learning how to recognize limiting beliefs and misleading thoughts and what to do about them is a great way for you to begin creating a healthier way forward in your life. This way, you can begin to control the thoughts that are creating feelings that are not serving you, or that are even harming you in some way. For example, if you find yourself consistently thinking thoughts that leave you feeling powerless and overwhelmed, you will feel powerless and overwhelmed often and this can lead to incredibly high-stress levels. Naturally, this is not healthy and this is a behavior that needs to be changed so that you can start experiencing healthier thoughts, emotions, and behaviors instead.

The best way to begin recognizing limiting beliefs is to recognize anytime you have held onto a belief that is causing you to feel or experience something that is unwanted. For example, if you find yourself thinking that you are incapable of achieving greatness in your favorite hobby because you only just started doing it, this might make you feel powerless and incapable of achieving your true goals. As a result, you might find yourself feeling demotivated to get anything done because you believe that you will not be able to do what you really want to do, anyway. However, if you were to recognize and change this limiting belief, you would be able to begin working on your chosen hobby and, inevitably, you would find yourself eventually creating the results that you truly desire.

Misleading thoughts are similar to limiting beliefs, except that they are less about what you believe and more about what you perceive. A misleading thought is essentially any thought you have that leads to you thinking the wrong thing about your environment or reality, to the point where you are significantly off from the truth. For example, if you are trying to learn a new hobby and you keep trying yet your results do not look like the results of someone who has mastered the hobby already, you might think that you are not making progress. You may wrongly think that you are bad at it, that you are doing something wrong, or that you are not showing big enough signs of improvement. Naturally, this is not true: the problem is that you are comparing yourself to someone who has already spent a lot of time mastering that particular craft.

The key in either scenario is to realize that your limiting beliefs or misleading thoughts are not ultimately true and that you are not required to continue thinking them. Then, you need to become curious about what the truth is so that you can start to identify a perception of your reality that is more likely to be true. For example, say you instead want to think that you are capable of becoming great at the hobby you like and you are making great progress. In order to support these new beliefs and thoughts, you would then want to create evidence that proves them to be true. So, you could begin to look at other people who have already mastered the craft and who started when you did. Or, you could look at your work against your past work to see how well you have improved already. This way, you can begin to compile evidence that proves to your mind that what your new beliefs and thoughts are is actually true and that you can comfortably believe in this reality instead.

This example shows how you can apply the process of changing limiting beliefs and misleading thoughts to a hobby specifically, but this process can be achieved for anything. If you want to create more self-discipline for yourself, improve your relationships, become better at something, feel less affected by something, or virtually anything else you can use the process of changing limiting beliefs and misleading thoughts to help you get there. Simply apply these same principles to your situation and watch as you begin to believe in something new, instead!

Eliminating Powerless Words from Your Vocabulary

As you begin changing your thoughts away from those that are associated with limiting beliefs and misleading thoughts, you need to also focus on your vocabulary and the way that you are speaking. Our words often reflect what we are thinking and reinforce it, meaning that we are ultimately proving to ourselves that what we think is true and that what we believe is also true.

Learning how to remove powerless words from your vocabulary forces your mind to begin thinking new thoughts and reinforces those new thoughts in your mind with ease. As a result, you are able to continue thinking these new thoughts effortlessly and with consistency.

Some of the powerless words you need to remove from your vocabulary include:

- "I can't"

- "I'm trying"

- "I don't want to"

- "But..."

- "I should..."

- "I need to"

- "I have to"

- "Maybe I will..."

- "Maybe I want to..."

- "I might..."

All of these words create a sense of doubt or powerlessness within yourself which ultimately leads to you creating a perception that prevents you from moving forward. As a result, you find yourself struggling to create the results that you desire to create in your life and you find yourself really struggling to become all that you can become. If you begin to remove these words from your vocabulary right away, chances are many of your limiting beliefs and misleading thoughts will quickly find their way out of your life, too.

Building Your Mental Strength and Motivation Through Thought

If your thoughts have such a huge impact on your ability to feel things, then naturally being able to control your thoughts means that you can have an even bigger impact on your ability to improve your mental strength and choose your emotions. As you learn how to control your thoughts or direct them on purpose, you will find that you actually have a massive capacity to create the experiences you want to create within your mind.

When it comes to directing your thoughts, you need to improve your ability to stay present and mindful about your environment and your experiences so that you can create your reality on purpose. The more present and mindful you are, the easier it will be for you to stay aware of your environment and choose your thoughts on purpose. This way, you can create your thoughts and shape what your perception is.

The key here is to start by becoming self-aware of your patterns, then of the actual moment. Then, you need to work on intentionally choosing what to focus on instead so that you can have the perception you want to have, rather than the perception that you feel forced to have.

As you start to become self-aware of your thoughts as they relate to your emotions, it will become easier for you to recognize what thoughts you are habitually having over and over again. Then, you can begin to identify when those thoughts are happening at the moment. Once you notice a thought happening at the moment that does not support you with staying motivated or creating the perception or feelings you want to have, you can intentionally start guiding it toward something else. For example, say you are thinking about how being in the car with someone else driving makes you feel anxious and it is hard for you to feel safe and comfortable with someone else behind the wheel. As long as you trust that this person is being safe, you can change your experience by choosing to focus on something else instead, such as the beautiful view outside, or the music on the radio. The key is to not think "I want to stop thinking about ____" and instead to think "I want to think about ____" and then focusing your entire attention and awareness on the new thought. This way, you are more likely to actually think it, internalize it, and keep it in your mind.

You can use this same redirection of your thoughts to create the emotions or motivation that you need in your life to help you get things done. The key is to always completely stop thinking about the thoughts that are no longer serving you and replace them with thoughts that are serving you so that you are thinking things that are actually helpful to and supportive of your new chosen experience.

THE BENEFITS OF EMOTIONAL INTELLIGENCE

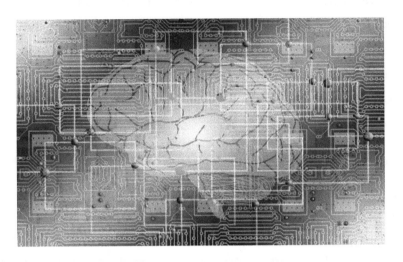

Conversation Skills

Part of improving emotional intelligence is not simply to improve yourself alone. Because none of us live in a vacuum, none of our emotional intelligence can occur without some outside influence, most likely with the people that we interact with every day. So not only will you be improving your emotional intelligence when you have conversations, but it is a continuous feedback loop that means that as your emotional intelligence increases, your conversation skills will also get better.

Studies show that communicators who have a higher emotional intelligence are exponentially more effective than those with a lower score. This is because a conversation is a two-way street that requires the participation of both people.

That is done most successfully when both participants are considerate of the feedback and information the other is giving them. As we already know, the ability to manage our own emotions as well as those of others is an important component of emotional intelligence. That means that in conversations, we will be using this skill to better understand the person we are talking with as well as altering how we talked with them to best, and most clearly communicate the message we are trying to convey.

This can present itself in many ways. People with higher emotional intelligence can have more difficult conversations without getting as flustered or overwhelm as their counterparts. This is because they can take in the situation, recognize, and manage those difficult emotions very quickly on the spot, before using their impulse control, send social skills to tactfully navigate those conversations.

Another way this presents itself is in leaving the other person feeling as if they were heard and understood during the conversation. Because you have learned how to show and communicate empathy as well as recognizing the healthy internal motivation to have that conversation, it allows you to eliminate some of your ego and commit to listening and hearing out the other person.

People Skills

One of the most sought-after benefits of emotional intelligence is very ambiguous but decidedly important people skills. It is hard to nail down exactly what it is, but it is definitely something that exists and improves with higher emotional intelligence.

Perhaps one element of having good people skills is that you are authentically yourself when you are around other people. This is something emotional intelligence can help you bring to fruition because you have done enough internal work to recognize the truth about yourself and how best to present those two other people. It also shows up because not only do you have empathy for other people, but you also have empathy for yourself and the difficult parts of yourself that you are still currently working on. Emotional intelligence helps you understand that you are a worthy and competent person who has something to gain by spending time with others; therefore, you know that your authentic self is the best version to put forth.

One way that this shows up is in maturity or level of assuredness in oneself. An emotionally intelligent person can show their improve people skills by the healthy relationships they have with others. Rather than seeing the world as a competition in which there can only be one winner, an emotionally intelligent person knows that they are not a victim, and there is no such thing as winning. Instead, everyone is winning in their way, and they are content with themselves and their journey in life. They have a worldview that is full of compassion for others as well as themselves, and therefore they are better able to connect with others.

Teamwork

Because emotional intelligence is so focused on navigating relationships with others, it only makes sense that people with higher emotional intelligence are also better at teamwork. This is because as difficult as it is to navigate the emotions and conversations with one other person when you are working on a team, you must do that same task but with every other person on the team, as well as the team as a whole.

The point of a team is almost always to accomplish some sort of goal together that wouldn't be able to be accomplished by just a single person. That means the team has a purpose for being together. As an emotionally intelligent person, you can recognize that this is an external motivation for the group. However, you also recognize that every individual has their own internal motivation for why they are participating. This knowledge can help you navigate any obstacles you may come up against as you work towards your goal.

A big part of the success of a team is dependent upon how engaged the members of the team feel in their work. This means that as individuals, everyone wants to know that they are important, and their work is crucial to the team's success. If they are being micromanaged or do not have very much flexibility or empowerment when it comes to how they do their job, this can result in them feeling as if they shouldn't be a part of a team, or that their efforts are not good enough. As an emotionally intelligent team member, you can recognize this either before it starts or once it has already begun, and attempt to resolve this issue.

When members of the team have high emotional intelligence, this can improve engagement by encouraging team members to work together to succeed rather than feel competition with their peers. A way that this can manifest itself is in teammates communicating frequently, clearly, and positively toward each other, encouraging each other, and celebrating the completion of smaller goals that work toward the end goal.

Leadership Skills

Most importantly, a high emotional intelligence gives you such a leg up when it comes to being a leader. Because you are in a role in which you are in charge of your employees, and you assigned the tasks that they spend most of their day on, it absolutely matters how you treat them, how you support their work, and how you respond to them. It is well understood that a happy employee is a productive employee. Your ability to appropriately communicate and celebrate the accomplishments of your team will go a long way in improving your leadership skills.

Having higher emotional intelligence will not only help you understand why it's important to be respectful to your employees and co-workers, but it will instill in you an innate sense of respect for others. This is crucial to keeping your employees satisfied and engaged, which has a direct correlation to their participation and success in work.

It also improves your leadership skills because you are more able to quickly adapt and change on the Fly. I do not know of many leadership roles that have no sudden situations that have to be dealt with or fires that need to be put out. Your ability to see the bigger picture, be aware of yourself and the team, regulate your own emotions and those of your team, and then implement a plan that keeps the long-term success in mind are all aspects of emotional intelligence.

EMOTIONAL INTELLIGENCE IN A RELATIONSHIP

Communicate

A relationship is most basically just two people who have decided, but they are important to each other. One of the most simple and impactful ways we can show another person they are important to us is by communicating with them. Whether that is taking time out at the end of every day to tell each other about how their day went, to be available to each other when an important or a difficult occasion arises, being able to communicate with each other is a crucial part of a relationship.

This also helps when it comes to communicating about your relationship. This could mean having the "what are we?"

conversation or "when should we have kids" discussion, and everything in between. What is important is that a relationship that is fulfilling has communicated boundaries and a shared vision. The only way you can achieve those is with a high level of emotionally Intelligent Communication.

It has also been shown that Partners who have engaging conversations with each other have a higher level of satisfaction in those relationships. This can be encouraged by participating in events together; that way, you have something to talk about. Specifically, trying something new to both of you together is very effective in creating not only new topics of conversation but also closer feelings of trust.

Empathy

When in a relationship with another person, you both must know that you are there for each other, and not simply in a one-sided relationship in which you expect everything from the other person and do not reciprocate to them. An important aspect of showing that you want to be equal Partners is using empathy.

This is more difficult than it sounds because we are all self-serving creatures. However, if you can show your partner that you do care about them outside of how it benefits you, that will go a long way in communicating to them your cared commitment. To show that you view both of you as equals and there needs and desires are as important as your own, you have to use empathy.

By stopping to listen to them, both the words they are saying, as well as the nonverbal communication they are using, you are showing them that they are important and that you want to have an understanding of how they feel. Everyone wants to feel as if their partner understands them, and truly here's what they are saying and what they mean.

Disagreements

Any healthy relationship is going to come into conflict or have a disagreement at some point in time, so you must know how to deal with this without it becoming overblown. Two people are invariably going to have different views on a situation, and this can be a great opportunity to learn about each other and grow together rather than become the ending point or a difficult situation in the relationship.

By using your emotional intelligence, you can't emphasize where your partner's coming from. Recognize both in yourself and them if this is a triggering situation that is going to cause a large emotional response and act accordingly. This might mean taking some time before discussing the situation, or it might mean simply recognizing and addressing that this has become a difficult topic, so both Partners can proceed gently.

It also requires a level of impulse control if you are feeling overwhelmed. By taking the space to hear out your partner rather than taking it as an attack to which you feel you have to reciprocate, you can self-regulate your emotions to grow from the situation.

Vulnerability

Because not all of us necessarily grew up with the best emotional role models in our lives, a lot of us have difficulties being vulnerable because we view them as weaknesses. It is a natural human instinct to protect our weaknesses to survive. The problem, however, is that emotional vulnerability is not something that is going to kill us, despite what are Primal instincts tell us.

To overcome this difficult obstacle and be vulnerable with our partner, we are communicating to them that we are being our fully authentic selves, and we trust them with our most difficult emotions. This is important to developing deep and personal relationships because, without a more intense level of self-disclosure, the relationship cannot be considered very close. This is something that should be reciprocated by both partners to show that they are on the same page about how intimate their relationship is, emotionally.

Honesty

An important aspect of having a healthy relationship is the ability to be honest with one another. Contrary to what many facetious people believe, this does not mean that you should say every mean thought that crosses your mind, but rather that you can be truthful in a respectful way at all times.

When people have a passing relationship or are simply friends or acquaintances, there can be a lot of tiptoeing around the truth to prevent any hurt feelings or misunderstandings.

When developing more personal relationships, it's is important that there is a level of trust that your partner does not want to hurt your feelings and acts accordingly. That means that when something comes up that they no might upset you, they do their best to communicate that to you in a gentle way.

That also means avoiding other unhealthy communication techniques such as not addressing the situation or using backhanded comments to beat around the bush. These are indicators that there is not a level of trust around emotions and being open to hearing difficult things.

Apologies

Perhaps the most difficult part of utilizing your emotional intelligence is admitting when you are wrong. However, this is a crucial step to ensuring your maturity and proving that you are using your skills. That being said, as you grow more practiced in all of your components of emotional intelligence, you will find it easier to admit when you are wrong and apologize.

This is a matter of understanding that your ego is not more important than the relationship itself. It is very common for a lot of us to want to be right about everything, but if that is taking the place of the emotions and well-being of your partner, then you need to start back at square one with learning emotional intelligence.

Part of coming to terms with being wrong and apologizing has to do with the impulse control that usually kicks in when your brain realizes you're wrong. Because your ego wants to protect itself, your brain goes into overdrive, coming up with excuses and blaming everything else that it can think of besides yourself. This is an opportunity for you to use your self-awareness to recognize this is a pattern and what you are feeling both physically and emotionally at that moment. It might take a lot of practice, but it is absolutely something that you can improve upon.

The great thing about being better at admitting you are wrong and apologizing is that you will not miss the sense of rightness you think you will be giving up. In fact, emotional intelligence helps you realize that it is not very important at all because you can better prioritize and contextualize the issue at hand. Rather than feeling a sense of resentment because you will apologize for things, you will actually feel a sense of freedom because you won't put as much importance on those things.

EMOTIONS IN BUSINESS – WHAT IS IT?

There is no exact date for the beginning of the era of behavioral economics, therefore we propose to consider the official frontier of 2002. Then for the first time in the entire history of the Nobel Prizes, the utmost distinguished accolade of the economic world - the prize in economics - was presented for research in the discipline of ... psychology. D. Kahneman was awarded the Nobel Prize for the use of psychological practices in economics. In his works, D. Kahneman demonstrated that resolutions made by people substantially deviate from the benchmark of the economic model. That is, when making a decision, people rarely are guided by their logical intelligence.

Logic does not play the first fiddle when a person evaluates the magnitude of the expected gains and losses and their probabilities. The degree of satisfaction from the acquisition, for example, $ 100 from a person is much lower than the degree of frustration from the loss of the same amount. Therefore, many are willing to take risks to avoid losses, but they are not inclined to take risks in order to gain profit.

The classical economy, which went into the world of a different work of D. Kahneman and his colleagues, suggested: a person is guided by elementary logic and his own benefit -

he buys where it is cheaper, works where he is paid more, he chooses one of two goods of the same quality that is cheaper.

D. Kahneman first introduced the concept of the human factor into economics and proposed to unite psychology and economics into one science. "People are guided not so much by logic, elementary arithmetic, as by emotions, by random impulses" - such an epitaph would be fair for the gravestone of the classical economy.

By the beginning of the third millennium, many sociologists and psychologists began to study and describe in detail the influence of emotions not only on an individual or a business environment but also on global processes in economics and politics. Perhaps the most vivid manifestation of this is the successful application of emotions in business. Careful and long-term observations of the acquisition of expensive things have shown: status goods are often bought impulsively, in order to get rid of the stressful state that indecision leads to. Purchases may be determined by snobbery, demonstrative reluctance to adhere to the same scale of quality indicators, as in the majority of group members. The demonstrative price is considered as payment for meeting the need to feel socially exclusive, to designate a high position in society at the expense of the right to own an expensive thing.

Our familiar businesswoman has been practicing "snobbery" in her New York boutique for a long time. The "cut-price" is set for high quality and quite standard things. And blouses, dresses, scarves are sold with a 200% margin.

On this platform and the desire to demonstrate their status a strategy of skimming is built, which manufacturers of various kinds of gadgets successfully use. At the same time, emotions help to sell not only luxury goods but also the most common goods from the mass segment. R. Eliot of Oxford University for more than five years studied the phenomenon, which he called shopping-addiction. He estimates that in the UK alone there are one million shopping addicts. Among them are people of any level of affluence. A separate category Oxford researcher identified as "vindictive customers." This group includes primarily housewives, whose husbands are successfully promoted through the ranks. Complementing the lack of male attention, these women are trying to remind their spouses of their existence with the reckless waste of money. Another group R. Eliot is referred to as "existential buyers": they revel in their own taste and assert themselves through purchases. One of the customers described this condition in such a way: "As I approach the store, I start to feel pleasantly excited. I adore human hum and color advertising. I plunge into the atmosphere of the supermarket and say to myself: "Relax and get high!"

The invisible hand of emotions is more and more clearly traced in the retail business, giving birth to forms of promotion of goods and services based on the understanding and use of emotions.

Natural intelligence and Emotional intelligence

Natural intelligence is largely genetically determined. Genetic inheritance is the most interesting, curious and highly controversial direction of modern science. Relying on the discoveries made in this direction, it can be said for sure that parents of musicians give birth to children with higher abilities to music. It is reliably known that in some areas of mathematics, for example, in arithmetic, success can largely depend on genetic factors. In general, being born with a good set of genes is great, but not everything. Because our natural intelligence develops. From birth, a person learns to perceive, memorize, form an idea about something, and finally - speak! And these processes, by the way, are far from simple and non-linear. Language develops; speech is shaped by natural intelligence.

On the basis of natural intelligence and speech, more and more complex intellectual operations are formed, which dramatically increase the possibility of intelligence. In other words, the conscious, purposeful and constant development of human intelligence may well compensate for the "starting" lag in the inheritance inherited from the parents or substantially increase the "parent capital."

General intelligence, based on abilities and using intellectual operations, provides to any of us the acquisition of knowledge, armed with which we successfully or not solve specific tasks in life. So, our intellect depends on a set of genes and the subsequent interaction with the external environment.

We all have emotions. This is our reaction to external stimuli and/or internal stimuli. As neuroscientists say, emotions are our responses, sewn into our brains. Our colleague, who visited Spain, loves to tell how, running away from the bull, he jumped a two-meter fence. When the horns of the bull were at his back, he threw his two hundred and forty-pound body through an enclosure with an incredible swing. "When I came to and looked around, I didn't believe that I had done it," he said. And rightly so. Because it was not he who did it, but his fear. Fear, joy, surprise and other emotions - this is an accelerator, clicking on which we multiply and accelerate our reactions. True, not every one of us knows how to press this almost magical pedal. And here it is time to report the good news: this can be learned. Intellectual control of emotions develops!

DISTINGUISHING BETWEEN FREEDOM AND DISCIPLINE

Swiss psychiatrist, Carl Jung, in one of his researches, described Individualism as development of one's consciousness. It is an identity- when a person carves out its uniqueness which is distinguished from society norm. The active word here is 'consciousness', 'self-realization' and 'personalization' whereby one becomes aware of their uniqueness. Jung notion applies to individuals as a member of group and not as an isolated existence.

Society plays an essential role in life experiences. In the experiment carried out by Jung, self-conscious individuals impressed a positive relationship with the group. Here, the self-conscious person allows himself to grasp the subconsciousness of the group and respond with intentional expression and manner.

Society provides institutions like family, schools and marriage, and not limited, so as to ensure the formation of individuality. The greatest threat for a person seeking individualism is conformity. Individualism will only manifest when one makes decision not because society demands the act but because he/she thinks the decision is right. The active word here is "choice". This requires a high level of confidence and responsibility which is unavoidable in both leadership and followership. Individualism is a most vital constitution of freedom.

Culture And Behavior Of Individualism

People's thoughts and behavior are highly influenced by culture. A factor in studying cross culture involves similarities between collective culture and that which is individualistic. Differences in both cultural formations are also significant in these studies.

In individualism, the culture is majorly influenced by an individual's value over a group/society. Here, an individual exerts his/her independence and maintains autonomy of power- The boss is self. The person's behavior depends less on society expectations and more on individual preferences. Western Europe are popular for its individualistic culture.

For example, the Pop-culture of a typical African-American musician living in Detroit is Rap/RnB. However, there are cases where other Genre, like classical music, are adapted by musicians of similar racial type and geolocation. This difference, although exists, are very few and it is greatly influenced by society institution, e.g. community groups like schools and faith organizations.

The table below shows the difference between Individualistic Culture and Societal Culture:

	Individualism	Society
1	Person's right take center stage	Society standards take center stage
2	Highest value placed on person's independence	Highest value placed on socialization
3	Person is more self-reliant	Person is socially dependent
4	Person is unique	Person conforms to society norm

The likelihood to focus attention on a person's identity is a pervasive aspect of culture which has a serious influence on the effectiveness of societal function. For example, a person who subscribes to individualism will often value their own culture and well-being over that imposed by the group. Unlike a Group's culture (collective culture) in which people make sacrificing of displeasing themselves for the benefit of everyone. This differences between individualism and society affects human behaviors in all sectors including career choices, product affiliation and responsiveness to social issues.

Cross-culture psychologist are now becoming very aware of the great influence that cultural/behavior have on a person's mental state and vice versa. However, an issue arises when individual preference/choice/culture may cause harm to the greater number of collectives/societies.

"It isn't what you have or who you are or where you are or what you are doing that makes you happy or unhappy. It is what you think about it." _ Dale Carnegie

Social Expectations and Social Norms

A society can be described as a group of people/individuals that are in continuous interactions socially and culturally. This group share a larger ideology aside which may or may not differ from personal ideals. These ideals could be formed politically, geographically, culturally or religiously. It could be affected by and not limited to class, race and even gender. The very essence of society structure is "grouping" individualism.

Society can influence one's behavior in many ways. The most common and predominant is the expectation of one's group/society. Often times, we expect others to act in a particular way and in a particular situation.

Often times, we expect others to act in a particular way and in a particular situation. Every society has an expected and proper way for people to behave. These expectations vary from one social group to another. A person in a particular group is expected to adopt these standard behaviors whether they like it or not. People often find it emotionally overwhelming to deal with such situations whereby how they feel about something is different about how society feels about it.

"All the worlds a stage,

And all the men and women merely players:

They have their exits and their entrances;

And one man in these times play many parts." _ William Shakespeare

What this poem captures are the social roles imposed by a single man. Imagine all the types of role you have to play in daily in your life. For example, a father, a mother, a son, an employee, a student, a friend, etc. every role has an expected way a person must behave which is referred to as social norm.

10 Most Popular Social Norms

1. One should be very popular and have a lot of friends
2. One must have a social media account and should remain active all the time.
3. One must be very good, an expert in fact, at some type of skill.
4. One should be doing something highly productive all the time.
5. One shouldn't be single but must be in a serious relationship that leads to marriage
6. One should be happy all the time and remain smiling always

7. One should plan to do certain types of things at a certain age e.g. graduate from university before age 25, get married before 30 and have a retirement plan before 60.
8. One should according to how they look and dress
9. On should have a particular type of view that is according to their family background and income.
10. One should be a graduate of a college or university

A high level of pressure exists where a person attains conformity to these unspoken/unwritten rules. Many of us are constantly dealing the right way to feel about these rules and whether we must accept conformity or not.

Society is a structure that has been in existence since the beginning of man. It has been, still is, and will be, the standard rule book, so it's impossible to act as though it doesn't exist. However, it must not be mandatory to follow these set of rules as long as it doesn't cause harm to others.

For example, in America, it is legal to own a gun but illegal to shoot a person just because one is having a bad day. However, the shooting can be justified in self-defense of the other being shot.

Understanding Human Rights and Freedom

Human rights are basic sets of freedom and choices owned by every person/human from the time of birth to the time of death. Its applicable irrespective of place of origin or religion. They are rights that cannot be taken away by any larger authority, only restricted, e.g. in criminal cases.

These set of rights have common values:

1. Dignity
2. Fairness
3. Respect
4. Independence

They are well defined and are protected by state law.

Identifying these values as rights of every member of the human race is the essence of peace and justice in the world.

a. Everyone is born equal and free with their own dignity and their rights. They are bestowed with consciousness and reasoning; therefore, they should act in respect amongst themselves in spirited brotherhood.

b. Everybody has rightful claims to the freedom stated here, and without any distinction of race, gender, color, language, sex, politics, birth place, social origin, status and property. There will be no distinction in respect to one's country's jurisdiction or international status; whether independently, non-self-governing or trust under other sovereignty.

c. Liberty, security of person and life itself is everyone's right.

d. Everyone is free from slavery or any form of servitude; the trade of slaves Is a crime in any form.

e. Everyone is free of any kind of torture to cruel and inhuman acts and treatments

f. All humans have the right to be recognized as a person by law.

g. Everyone is equal by law and entitled to be equally protected by the law without any discrimination.

h. All have equal right to efficient remedy by national tribunals for taking actions that violates the basic rights given to him by the law.

i. All is free from becoming subjects of arbitrary arrests, exile or detention.

j. All has equal entitlement to fair and public hearing from both independent tribunal and impartial tribunal, in deciding whether his obligation and any crime charged against him.

k. All who are charged with a criminal offense are by right, innocent, and should be treated as such before proven guilty by the public trial in which he is guaranteed all necessary defense.

l. None should let interference of their privacy, home, family or correspondence. There shouldn't be an attack on one's honor either. All have equal right to be protected by law against all kinds of such attack.

m. Everybody has their rights to move freely and where to reside in state borders. Anybody can leave their country and visit any country.

n. If persecuted, anyone can seek and enjoy a foreign country's asylum. This right is not invoked when persecutions are genuinely risen in cases that are not politically related.

o. Everybody has an equal right to have a nationality. No one should be denied tier nationality or changing their nationality.

p. With no limitations like nationality, race or religion, all ag
appropriate men and women have a right to marriage and
to build their family. They are guaranteed equal marriage
rights during marriage and after its dissolution. Marriage
will only be allowed if both parties are willing and none
must be forced to their will. Family is naturally the
primary group segment of society. It must be protected by
state and society.

q. Everybody can own properties on their own and in
relation to others. No one must be deprived of his
properties.

r. Freedom of conscience, and of thoughts, and of religion is
given as an equal right to everybody. This includes the
freedom to make changes on one's beliefs or religion. And
freedom to teach others these beliefs whether in private in
public and to make these beliefs into practice of worship
and of observation.

s. Everybody is rightfully entitled to freely express
themselves and their opinions; whether seeking or
receiving information by any media, and without
interference.

t. Everybody is entitled to peaceful assembly and
association.

u. Everybody is entitled to partake in governing his country,
whether directly or by choosing freely, a representative.
All has their rights to partake in public services of their
country.

v. Everybody who is a member of a social group, has a right to security of society and given freedom to access these securities.

w. Everybody as his freedom to work and choice of employment/career. He must receive a favorable terms/conditions of employment and to be protected against unemployment. Everybody, irrespective of discrimination, must be given equal Wages of labor. All are entitled to become a member of any trade union to protect their own interest.

x. Everybody is entitled to live in their own standards for the well-being of themselves and their family which includes the kinds of food, housing and clothing, medical care and all other social and public services.

y. Everybody is entitled equal rights to education

z. Everybody can freely partake in their community culture and enjoy and share artifacts.

Self-Will And Self-Discipline

A self-willed person is one is unmindful of other's will and wishes. More often than not, society sees a self-willed person as unreasonable, dominant or stubborn. They are quite challenging to deal with because of their focus on themselves and their decisions. Their selfishness doesn't come from a greed to put their well-being in first- a self-willed person may be a martyr. However, their selfishness is from an ardent desire to follow what they think is the right path.

The will power of a self-willed person is conscious, determined and exert. This will could be described in 3 main categories:

I WILL this gives one the determination to venture into something without losing interest or giving up. It is what puts a person on a treadmill rather than letting the person stay idle on the couch.

I WON'T POWER this is the power to resist temptation. This power comes to play when on chose not to eat ice-cream and chocolate if the goal is to lose weight.

I WANT POWER it gives a long-term influence of one's decision. It is the power that focus on delay of gratification. The famous experiment carried by Stanford marshmallow shows that people who delay gratification are better off than those with instant gratification.

First thing to consider while identifying a self-willed person;

1 Independence go a long way when becoming self-willed. A person will address issues in a unique and different path. She loves a challenge and she invent new ways to solve them. If they get to a point of needing assistance, they will openly and ask. There is strength in admitting fault. A strong-willed person is not afraid of other people's thought about him because he only values' his thoughts and opinions.

2 To be self-willed, one must be thoughtful about most things. Their minds are rich with information about almost anything because they are constantly learning about these things. They analyze events on emotions and take sufficient effort to act on it. They are constantly putting puzzle pieces together-in different forms of interest like in businesses or politic, and to make sense of what is going on. They are wildly imaginative they are the creators of extraordinary ideas.

3 They are inquisitive about their surroundings and so they question every rule set by society. It doesn't necessarily mean that they are law breakers, it simply means that they are aware of their human rights. they don't tolerate when they are taken for granted.

4 They are very passionate about their interests. They will go the extreme to achieve their goals and vision because they are not easily afraid of a challenge. They have the fix-it mentality which in most cases, optimistic. They are persistent in their endeavors.

5 They are the most faithful, loyal and trustworthy. Self-willed people have a high moral and they care genuinely for loved ones. They only trust few people so they try to stick with the selected few. These people are truthful and honest and because they believe in their moral conducts, they have no reason to hide them for others opinion.

6 They place high value on their freedom and personal space. A Self-willed person don't like interference when making their own decisions. They need time and space to meditate which involves taking a break from the crowd once in a while. This person trusts his instinct and let their voice lead them.

7 The biggest critic of a strong-willed person is himself. This makes them consistently improving on themselves because they are aware of being better. This owes to the fact they place high self-esteem. They don't hesitate to admit to failure hence they re-strategize to turn failure to success even though it takes a longer time (i.e. the concept of failing forward).

8 A self-willed person says less and do more. They only say what they will do. They are straight forward and direct with their speech. They only speak up after they had gathered their thoughts which gives their words credibility. This means that their choices are often right than none.

Self-willed and strong-willed are one in the same. To become strong-willed, one must first discover self and trust in self. However, a self-willed person must exercise self-discipline in order to maintain a steady mental state.

Mastering self-discipline

A very important skill for leadership is self-discipline. This is essential and effective in daily life and how one deals with events. Although, while everyone acknowledges its power, only few people are experts in exercise it.

What is self-discipline?

It is an inner source of power that fuel's one decision and compels one to follow them thoroughly. It is a control of thought, action and emotions. This is important in all types of leaderships because it enables a leader to stick to decisions without changing minds. It makes perseverance look easy, which indicates a high sense of positivity and self-esteem. A leader knows that he will succeed, therefore puts in will-power. Feelings that are distracting by nature: addiction, laziness and procrastination, can have no significance in the lives of sufficient self-discipline.

Daily challenges are unavoidable and handling them properly means ensuring that it doesn't upset our health and well-being of both self and the environment. In all type of strategy/tactics in dealing with problems, it is important to exercise patience, persistence and perseverance.

The lack of this skill leads to loss and failure. E.g. a person must have mastered self-discipline in overcoming negative habits like smoking, over-eating, relationship problem, else the person will never achieve goal.

Other Advantages of self-discipline;

- It lets one not to act on impulse
- It helps to fulfil promises made to self and others
- It overcomes procrastination
- It gives extra drive even after the initial rush of enthusiasm to start a project
- It wakes one early so to utilize the limited hours of the day.

HOW TO DEVELOP SOCIAL SKILLS AND The Art Of Listening

How To Improve Your Social Skills?

To continue increasing your EQ, you need to grow your social skills as well because only by actively engaging with others can you strengthen your bond with them, get insight into their emotions, and learn to influence and lead them positively.

Here is how you can achieve these goals.

Be Cordial with People

When in a social situation, always be on your best behavior and be amicable with everyone around you. Engage politely with people, greet them nicely, and make sure you smile as much as you can—obviously not in a fake manner.

Also, try doing little favors for people like fetching someone a drink or letting someone take the last appetizer off the platter when you were trying to grab it as well. Little gestures go a long way in strengthening relationships and making you come off as the bigger and cordial person.

Appreciate Others

Appreciating others is a surefire way to create a home in the hearts of those you care for. When you compliment someone or appreciate their efforts, you encourage the person and make them feel good. This creates a soft corner for you in the person's heart, thereby bringing the two of you together. Look for something you can appreciate in every person around you, particularly those you wish to influence and build better relationships with. You will definitely interact much better.

Listen to Others

An incredibly effective way to draw people towards you is to lend them a keen ear that listens to all their concerns, ideas, worries, suggestions, and stories. When conversing with someone, especially a person you wish to influence and draw closer to you, allow them to speak more and listen to their stories with keen interest. Maintain direct eye contact, ask relevant questions and stop fidgeting with your phone or watch. The more attention you pay to someone talking, the more invested you become in the conversation and the stronger you pull the person towards you. This works really well for making your partner fall in love with you again as well as impressing business associates.

Build a Signature Communication Style

Everyone has their own preferences and communication styles when it comes to conveying their ideas, thoughts and concepts. If you want to be in a more commanding position or want others to view you as an influencer, develop a unique communication style. What is your main communication medium? Do you emphasize more on verbal or nonverbal communication?

Identify a Common Ground

When you find people switching off from a conversation or not responding favorably to what you are saying, switch to another topic. Find a common ground between you and the other person to establish a comfort level. People in sales use this communication technique all the time. They are trained in the art of building a rapport with potential customers.

Focus on Building Strong Relationships While Being Professional

Of course, there is scope for speaking about non-work related things with coworkers. That's what bonding and a happy work atmosphere/family is all about. We want to bond and find common links with people we work with. Everyone seeks to connect with people they work with. Getting personal sometimes helps break barriers and make us see people as humans with feelings and not just coworkers, subordinates or bosses.

Stay Positive

Even when you have to communicate a not so pleasant message, keep it positive and constructive. The aim should always be to resolve the issue or obtain better results. Being aggressive, hurting someone or making them feel embarrassed may not necessarily give you better results in future. However, a more positive approach will may help results in a manner you never imagined.

Say The Right Things at The Right Time

This is one of the most important pointers when it comes to communicating with people in a professional capacity. Sometimes, the issue in communication doesn't arise based on how something is being said; it is simply about when it is said. If you have an issue with someone at work, address it to them directly rather than letting the entire workplace know about it. Similarly, everyone has their bad days and moments. Show more empathy towards people by understanding them. We all get stressed and have our share of unproductive or inefficient days. It is alright to reach out to people and make allowances for them when they are clearly having a bad time.

Talk to People In Their Language

Always use language that resonates with your people. If you are dealing with a bunch of interns, avoid using too much technical jargon that they may not understand or identify with. They may identify with a slightly breezier and millennial lingo. Similarly, if you are addressing a bunch of senior management personnel, you may have to resort to a more technical and professional language that resonates with them.

Use Humor

This is one of the lesser known secrets that are used by successful professionals while communicating with their employees. Try and inject humor into your conversation to make it more memorable, entertaining and impactful. Humor helps disarm people, and makes the flow of communication and discussion more fluid.

Mastering Basic Social Skills

Social skills are not just about the way we communicate with each other. You need to build empathy to improve the way that you connect with others, which will prove to be an especially useful skill in a lot of social situations. People skills are - you guessed it - another word for social skills. At work, being great at your job is only going to take you so far. To climb the career ladder is going to require you to have an extra set of skills on your hands, which is to be seen as a people person, someone sociable and likeable, a leader that other employees will be willing to follow.

Whether you're an introvert or otherwise, there are a few techniques you could master to take your social game up a notch so you can learn to handle any social situation and come out on top:

- Call Them by Name - When a person hears their name being mentioned by someone else, their attention is immediately piqued.

- Tone Change - If you notice one thing about charismatic speakers, it is that their tone of voice is always changing.

- Gesture with Your Hands - When 760 people were surveyed after they had watched Ted Talks equivalent to 100 hours showed that there was a direct correlation between hand gestures and the number of views the video received.

- Maintaining Eye Contact - According to Aberdeen University psychologists, maintaining the right amount of eye contact can make you appear more attractive and likeable.

- Smiling - A charismatic person's smile is relaxed, natural and at ease, warm, genuine, and friendly.

Developing Good Listening Skills

Today, nearly everything is high-speed, high-tech, and of course, high-stress. We've got a lot of stimuli going on that our emotions are more easily triggered than ever these days. Communication, social, and emotional intelligence skills are equally more important today because of this.

Real, honest to goodness listening and tuning into not just others, but ourselves has become a rare thing these days, but it is just what we need to flourish. EI, communication and social skills aid with conflict resolution, building genuine relationships and understanding, and problem solve in a way that IQ never can do quite so accurately. Effective listening skills, in particular, is a skill that needs to be worked on.

A common communication barrier - which frequently occurs these days - is when someone decides to reach a decision or course of action without fully listening to all the information at hand. Making assumptions can lead to complications because when you are not well informed, you run the risk of making more mistakes than you should.

Being able to listen effectively is also part of the effective communication process. Both the communicator and the receiver must be able to listen effectively to one another while each is expressing their points of view.

Relevant and important information is in danger of being missed if you are not able to listen well to what the communicator is trying to say to you. And in the case of the communicator, they would also need to be able to listen to the feedback that they are receiving if they hope to improve their communication skills moving forward. Developing effective listening abilities is the loose end that ties everything else (EI, communication, and social skills) together.

How To Improve Your Social Skills?

Listen Carefully to Others

Listen to their words, but also observe and give careful attention to non-verbal language. Body language is the key. How is a person holding their self physically? What does their posture look like? What are they doing with their hands? Do they look comfortable or tense? Many psychologists say that micro-expressions, or minute expressions of the face and facial expressions, are more telling than the actual words someone is saying. When you are focusing on someone and you want to better understand their feelings, it's important to consider many different verbal and non-verbal cues.

Start to Empathize

When you understand what emotions, someone is feeling by listening and observing them as described above, that's a good first step. But if you want to gain insight into why they are feeling that way, you must try to understand their point of view. Imagine how you would feel in the situation they're going through. Whether it's physical, emotional, financial, whatever, you can only empathize with the other person if you leave the safe bubble you are in and then attempt to put yourself in their shoes. Visualize what their problems are, and how you would react in such a way.

Reflecting on Your Emotions

After you have successfully empathized with a person, that's when the reflection process begins. You have to reason with the emotions you have felt by empathy and put a label on them cognitively. Is the other person sad or depressed? Are they angry or humiliated? How are they responding to the situation they're in, and is it reasonable? Is this a dangerous emotion?

Interact with People Different Than You

If you are constantly surrounded by the same people, you will have difficulty learning to read new social cues and how other people relay their feelings. Try and expand your horizons and interact with new people – whether it's in your social circle of friends or work colleagues.

HOW EMOTIONAL INTELLIGENCE AFFECTS YOUR LEADERSHIP

Naturally, you didn't just come here to learn about what emotional intelligence is and what makes for a great leader. You came here to learn about how you can embrace the skill of emotional intelligence to help make you a great leader. Right? For that reason, it is ideal that we dig into what it means to be a great leader using the power of emotional intelligence.

Emotional intelligence is going to help you improve your leadership skills in many different ways, primarily because emotional intelligence skills overlap directly with what it truly takes to become a great leader. With that being said, if you want to become a great leader, you need to learn how to engage in emotional intelligence to improve the skills that will support you in becoming a great leader.

Self-Awareness and Self-Regulation

Self-awareness and self-regulation are two cornerstones for emotional intelligence, and they also happen to be two important elements of leadership. As you learn how to become self-aware and learn how to self-regulate, you will find yourself improving your leadership qualities in that you can begin to become aware of how your own actions impact your leadership skills and your team. When you have a clear picture of what your strengths and weaknesses are, you can lead your team with humility and allow your team to all come together to add their own unique strengths and weaknesses to the mix.

Self-awareness itself is also going to help you understand how your own emotional experiences, reactions, and responses will affect the people around you. As a leader, this means that you are going to have an easier time understanding how you can adjust your own responses to various situations so that you can continue to lead your team with greatness. If a leader struggles to identify and respond appropriately when they are feeling emotional, they will find themselves struggling to lead their team because they will not be able to manage the emotions of the entire team. While it is important that leaders know how to assert boundaries around emotional experiences to avoid taking on the emotions of everyone on their team, having an increased awareness of these responses helps them engage in a stronger manner. This way, they are able to acknowledge and communicate their needs with some level of emotional urgency without creating too much stress or overwhelm for their team.

Self-regulation is a large part of being able to be self-aware and respond appropriately, too. When you are able to self-regulate, this is when you are really able to take that self-awareness and turn it into a trigger that prompts you into action so that you can begin to make strong changes that are on part with emotional intelligence.

As a leader, self-regulation is important for far more than just knowing how to identify your emotions and manage them properly. Self-regulation will also ensure that you do not verbally attack others, including your team, that you do not rush or make impulsive decisions, that you do not stereotype people, and that you do not attempt to push people to go against their values. When you can self-regulate as a leader, you ensure that you are able to lead in a way that is impactful, effective, and respectful to everyone that you are leading.

Motivating Yourself and Your Team

Leaders who have strong EQ do not only know how to diffuse unwanted or difficult emotions; they also know how to create and navigate excited emotions. Knowing how to motivate yourself and your team is a cornerstone skill in being able to become a great leader, and it is also a skill that is largely associated with emotional intelligence. When you have the capacity to motivate yourself and your team, you create the opportunity for you to keep each of you effectively moving toward your goals rather than having everyone procrastinate or struggle to keep moving forward.

As you learn how to engage in emotional intelligence, you learn about what it takes to motivate you to keep going. You learn this by first learning about what it takes to actually motivate and inspire you into action so that you are likely to stay devoted to getting tasks done. You also learn this by learning how to delay gratification so that you are less likely to be emotionally driven by instant gratification and more likely to be rationally driven by the idea of experiencing greater rewards in the future. When you learn about how you can delay gratification by self-regulating and managing your own emotions, then you really learn how to motivate yourself and stay inspired to see things through.

As a team leader, motivating yourself is only the first step. Knowing how to motivate yourself will ensure that you can stay enthusiastic and prepared to hype yourself up and keep yourself going toward any goal that you have set with your team. The next part of knowing how to create motivation and inspiration to work toward goals is knowing how to motivate your team members.

Part of being emotionally intelligent is knowing about how other people's emotions work and learning how to read other people's emotions. Through this, you can find ways to inspire and motivate your team into action so that they are likely to want to work toward attempting to achieve the goals you have set out for your team, too. In order to do this, you are going to need to know about what it takes to really, truly motivate your team in every possible way.

When you can effectively stay motivated and motivate your team, your team morale is boosted, and you are all a lot more likely to achieve your goals. Motivating your team will often be as much about building energy as it will be about maintaining positive energy in your work environment, all of which ultimately falls down to the leader and what culture the leader is capable of facilitating for the team.

Having Empathy for Your Team

Having empathy for your team is an important part of creating team morale, motivating your team, keeping your team inspired, and collectively working toward achieving your goals. As a leader, empathy means that you can put yourself in the situation of your team members and understand what they are going through. Empathy is going to provide you with two crucial things as a leader: the ability to create better relationships with your team members, and the ability to come up with solutions for how you can still succeed while being kind to your team members.

When it comes to having better relationships, being empathetic means that your team knows that you understand where they are coming from and that you have compassion for what they are going through. When you can be empathetic toward your team, you can create a stronger bond with them, which ultimately helps them feel more supported and encourages them to want to work together with you on your team more. When people feel supported, connected, and cared for, this naturally elevates their level of commitment and motivation, which leads to them having a much deeper desire to truly want to help work toward the bigger picture.

In addition to helping your team members feel more connected and supported, knowing how to be empathetic for your team means that you can also find creative ways to keep your team on track with your goals even when one of your team members is struggling with something. When you can be empathetic, you can identify what that team member needs, what is going to help them feel supported as they work, and how you can create a plan for them to still complete their work without driving themselves into burnout.

When you are able to empathetically create new solutions for your team members to continue working toward their goals, two things happen: they become more committed to the team, and their productivity levels go up. Because you have taken the time to care about them and make their wellbeing a commitment for you as their leader, they begin to care more about what you are leading toward. As a result, they are more likely to become emotionally invested in creating the results your team is looking for, which means that they are going to find themselves truly working their best as often as they can. As well, because you have modified the task to support them in their time of need, they are more likely to be able to get the job done because they are not attempting to fight back against things which may be keeping them in a state of resistance. Through these two shifts, you make it far easier for your team to become more deeply connected and to succeed at creating the results you are looking for.

Improved Leadership-Oriented Social Skills

As a leader, you must have excellent social skills, or you are going to struggle to connect with and lead your team. Team leaders who lack social skills find themselves having difficulty building relationships with and therefore motivating their team because they are unclear about what it takes to receive the trust and commitment of their team members. Improved social skills mean you are far more likely to actually earn the trust and respect of your team members, which means you will naturally be able to encourage them to have the same goals as you so that you can mutually reach your team goals.

As a team leader with a high EQ, you will be able to navigate conflict with greater ease, improve your communication skills in general, motivate people, praise others in a way that makes them feel good, inspire others, and become more charismatic in general. Through this, you will find yourself having a much easier time navigating social situations and creating a stronger sense of commitment and devotion from within your team.

Two of the most important social skills listed here that we have not yet talked about include conflict resolution and your ability to praise others in a way that helps them feel good and inspires them to take bigger action. When you know how to engage in these two important practices with ease, you massively increase your "pull" as a leader, which means you have a greater ability to encourage your team to stay motivated and work toward your bigger goals.

Conflict resolution is an extremely important task as a leader. As a leader, you are going to experience times where you have a conflict with your team members, where you have conflict with people outside of your team, where your team members have conflict with each other, and where your team members have a conflict with other people. Knowing how to mediate this conflict and support your team members with being able to resolve these conflicts means that you can improve the likelihood of you and your team members being able to proceed after conflict has risen.

When it comes to conflict resolution, there are many skills that need to be addressed, which you will learn about later in this book. Ultimately, the goal, however, is to identify the emotions of everyone involved and use this knowledge as a way to deescalate the emotional situation and bring everyone involved to a resolution that works for everyone.

As an emotionally intelligent leader, you also need to increase your capacity to learn how to praise people on your team in a way that supports them with their growth. When you can praise people properly, you encourage them to continue doing a great job, increase their loyalty to your team, and support them with their own self-confidence.

When it comes to praising people, it is important that you do so in a proper manner, however. Especially as a team leader, you will need to learn how to give praise in a way that encourages people, builds their confidence, and helps everyone on the team feel encouraged to do better. As a team leader, it is also especially important that you learn how to give praise without being biased or picking favorites. You need to make sure that you are using praise to build up everyone on your team equally to ensure that everyone is feeling supported and as though they are an important part of your team. This way, they are all far more likely to do even better and support one another, rather than developing jealousy or complacency because they feel like they cannot do anything wrong, or like they cannot do anything right.

Improved Leadership Skills in General

Emotional intelligence is going to improve your leadership skills in general, as well. When you increase your emotional intelligence, you will find that your skills directly related to improving your leadership and your skills related to other areas of your life improve, too. This way, you are far more likely to become a strong leader, not just for your team but in every way in your life. As a result, you are going to be far more likely to create what you desire in your life.

One of the biggest ways you are going to find emotional intelligence really improving your leadership skills outside of directly improving your leadership skills is through your ability to improve your interactions with life in general. Due to your improved social skills, ability to manage your health, relationships, intrapersonal skills, and emotional management skills in general, you will find that you have a much easier time managing yourself. As a result, you will find that you are less likely to bring stress or outside problems or experiences into your leadership style, which means that you will be more likely to lead in an objective and grounded manner.

CHARISMATICALLY EMPHATIC

We all long to relate to others on a deeper level—one that goes beyond just surface relationships. To feel that deep bond and connection with others is a gift that is made possible through empathy.

We relate to the way others are feeling by observing their body language, the tone of their voice, and opening ourselves to being aware of the emotional energy that vibrates between them and us.

Fine-tuning your empathy skills will give you not only the ability to feel what the other person does but to assess what they need.

You know when they need comfort, and you know when they need support.

You know when they need attention, and you can sense when they might need you to step back and give them some space.

But could too much empathy be a bad thing?

Empathy and Its Relation to Stress

Too much empathy can be a bad thing when it starts to affect you more than it should.

With empathy, you're trying to experience what the other person is going through, which means if they feel stressed, so do you. If they feel anxious or angry, you feel the same.

Depending on your skills, you might even be able to feel their physical pain, not just the emotional pain alone, and if you absorb these emotions into your body and allow them to linger, they could start to hijack your body and mind emotionally.

When you take on someone else's emotions, you become susceptible to feeling unhappy or miserable. Handling emotions can be a draining ordeal, and when you have to deal with the emotions of others on top of your own, your energy levels can quickly start to deplete.

Empathy, when left unbridled, could potentially lead to a spike in your cortisol levels, which then makes it more difficult for you to manage your emotions.

When you allow other people's emotions to affect you, you start to feel responsible for them, and you want to help them overcome their pain. You start feeling stressed about what you can do to help them feel better.

But the thing is, if you try to help them too much, you might come off as intrusive, even if your intentions may be good.

Some people just want someone who will listen to them, and if you try to help, they might feel uncomfortable, possibly even embarrassed.

In some cases, they might even feel like you're imposing or being disrespectful when you try to do too much, believing that you're "helping" them.

This eventually starts to affect your relationship when they pull away and try to distance themselves because they no longer feel comfortable expressing themselves to you.

When they start to pull away, that just adds to your stress over possibly losing a relationship.

Understanding Stress

> "It's not the load
> that breaks you down,
> it's the way you carry it."
>
> — Lou Holtz

Feeling worried, drained, and overwhelmed. Those feelings are generally associated with "stress."

Its technical definition is "any emotion which is an uncomfortable experience, followed by a predictable biochemical which causes behavioural and physiological changes."

Capable of affecting those as young as little kids, stress knows no age limitations. Nor is it restricted to one specific gender alone, as both men and women can feel equal amounts of stress.

This emotion can be so powerful that it is capable of causing both psychological and physical problems if experienced for a prolonged period.

Not all stress is bad, though—sometimes, it can prove to be useful. There are times when you might need stress to give you that extra boost in motivation so that you, in turn, are spurred to action.

When you feel the stress of exams drawing close, that causes you to get your act together, buckle down, and start studying intensely. Or when you've got an imminent deadline at work coming up, feeling stressed about it encourages you to focus long enough to get things done because you know you have to.

It's just when stress is experienced in extreme amounts does it become a problem, since there are potential health consequences that follow.

Why experiencing chronic stress is bad for you is because it's persistent. Over time, the weight of this negative emotion is going to be debilitating both mentally and physically.

Chronic stress is not like your daily stressors that can easily be managed and regulated with a couple of healthy management techniques.

When left untreated, chronic stress leads to serious health conditions like insomnia, anxiety, muscular aches and pains, high blood pressure, and even a weaker immune system.

There's even research to suggest that chronic stress could potentially cause depression, obesity, and major illnesses like heart disease.

Stress is a very serious condition that needs to be paid attention to. Yet, the American Psychological Association's survey indicates that at least 33% of Americans still don't talk about the different ways they can control their stress with a healthcare professional.

Stress can affect you in a serious way, and no one is spared in this case.

Some people are capable of coping with it more effectively than others, and stress could have any number of triggers that cause it too. Family and work pressure, relationship pressure, the pressure of dealing with schoolwork, and managing financial responsibilities are all potential triggers.

It could even be triggered by a sudden major change in your life that's negative, like when you or someone you know has fallen ill, or you've lost your job, had a relationship come to an end and more. Even traumatic incidences like an accident or a natural disaster is a potential stress trigger.

One of the hardest forms of stress to detect, however, is routine stress.

When you have become so accustomed to stress being part of your routine, your body doesn't know how to signal anymore when something isn't quite right. Let it go on long enough, and that's when health issues start to crop up.

Not everyone tends to experience stress the same way either.

For some people, stress can result in digestive problems, while others may experience headaches and muscle tension as a side effect. Since the immune system is weakened by stress, it's easier for those who deal with chronic stress on a regular basis to be more susceptible to viral infections like the common cold or flu.

As debilitating as it may be, there are ways for you to manage and regulate your stress levels.

Like your emotions, you can keep them under control with the following stress-management techniques:

- Recognize when your body is signalling signs of stress.

- Once you've identified your condition, speak to your doctor or health care professional about it.

- A natural way to keep stress under control is to get at least 30-minutes of exercise or physical activity several times a week.

- Immerse yourself in relaxing activities once, twice, maybe three or more times a week (depending on what that activity is). Meditation and yoga, for example, are something you can do daily at home.

- Connect with the people in your life who matter most, because they can provide you with the support (emotional or otherwise) that you need to help you manage your stress levels.

- When it starts to feel like too much, seek help from a professional. If you're dealing with depression and find yourself experiencing the occasional suicidal thoughts, seek professional help immediately.

Improving Your Charisma and Self-Discipline

Charisma and self-discipline, the two other traits you need to help you relate to others and keep your emotions in check.

To succeed in business, learn how to manage people and become a great leader, boosting your EQ skills alone is just one part of it.

You need charisma for your social skills and self-discipline that lets you remain in control no matter what social setting you find yourself in.

Let's look at the characteristics of a charismatic leader first.

Charisma and Charm

> "Charisma is a sparkle in people that money can't buy. It's an invisible energy with visible effects."
>
> — Marianne Williamson

A common misconception is that charisma is part of your nature, and who you are as a person.

What a lot of people don't realize is that charisma is actually more about the way you carry yourself, and the things that you say and do.

Charisma and charm and personality traits that you can create for yourself, and that is one of the many secrets and techniques successful people have put into play.

Just like everything else they have, they put in the work for it, and they built up their charisma if they weren't naturally born with it.

Why?

Because they knew it could be done.

Some people are naturally charismatic individuals, but if you aren't one of those, there's no reason why you can't become one.

How much do you know about charismatic and charming people so far?

They're likeable for one thing, but you can't quite explain precisely why they are so likeable.

They have a certain je ne sais quoi that you can't quite put your finger on.

They seem to have an aura that just kind of flows out of them that people become drawn to.

That's the magic of charisma.

Like everything else we've been learning so far, working on your charismatic abilities going to take some work before you build up to it, but adopting these techniques will give you a good head start:

- Be Comfortable Physically - One of the most overlooked approaches to exuding confidence, charm, and charisma is being comfortable physically.

It's awfully hard to pay attention and put your best self forward when you're distracted by how itchy, tight or uncomfortable your clothing may be.

It's important to wear clothes that fit well, and something that you are comfortable in. You won't just look better—you'll feel much better, too.

- Don't Fidget - You're going to make everyone else uncomfortable when you're fidgeting all the time.

It sends a signal that you're not comfortable, or that you'd rather be anywhere else but here right now. Pay attention, stay focused, and be present and attuned to what's going on around you.

- Don't Blurt It Out - Charismatic people understand the importance of thinking before you speak out loud.

That's how they minimize the moments when they feel like putting their foot in their mouth.

One wrong word or sentence is all it takes to put people off instantly—and once that happens, it is often an uphill battle to try and regain favour in their eyes.

Conversations that happen will leave a lasting impression about you, about the way you've carried yourself and the things which you said.

Your mind needs to be working twice as fast to process the information you're receiving from the other person, and quickly analyze the things you plan to say to make sure it's appropriate before you speak.

- The 2-Second Pause - Instead of immediately jumping to respond, pause for 2-seconds before you reply.

This helps with the whole "think before you speak" scenario, too.

When you jump in right away as soon as the other person has stopped talking, they might get the impression that you weren't paying attention to them, and you were busy formulating a response in your mind instead (which you were probably doing).

- Provide Meaningful Answers - If you want the conversation to develop into something more, you're going to have to play your role beyond just asking the right questions.

You're going to have to learn to give meaningful answers too when you are asked a question by the other person.

Ideally, questions should bounce back and forth between you and the other person.

Asking the right questions is a good thing, but returning meaningful answers is even better because people will be curious and interested in knowing more about you the same way you are interested in getting to know them.

- Be Approachable - Start off on the right foot immediately by doing this one, very simple thing – make yourself approachable.

You don't even have to do much except to keep an open body language and smile with sincerity.

Relax, don't hunch to make it appear you're uncomfortable, don't cross your arms in front of you (it signals that you're closed off to other people), look around interestedly and smile openly with anyone you happen to make eye contact with.

- Don't Underestimate a Smile - A smile is the best body language ice-breaking weapon everyone possesses at their disposal.

It lights up your face entirely. If the other person is feeling ill at ease, they would immediately start to relax when they see how warm and friendly you appear to be—conversations are more inclined to start off on a positive note.

- Remain Positive - Even if the emotions you're feeling are anything but positive at that moment.

People are put off by negativity. Nobody wants to engage in small talk with someone who is constantly complaining about everything.

If you wouldn't like being around someone like that, avoid doing the same thing.

If you're having a bad day and need to blow off a little steam, it is best not to engage in small talk with anyone if your head isn't in the right place.

Always keep it positive, it is very important to be friendly, upbeat, and cheerful when you're small talking with anybody so that they leave with a good first impression about you.

- No Rush Between Sentences - It's not a race.

There's no need to let off a stream of verbiage one after another because you're afraid that awkward silences may follow.

Firing off one topic after another and question after question makes the other person feel uncomfortable, too, like they're being interrogated or something.

Self-Discipline and Persistence

> "Leaders aren't born they are made.
> And they are made just like
> anything else, through hard work.
> And that's the price we'll have
> to pay to achieve that goal,
> or any goal."
>
> — Vince Lombardi

Having the intention to become a more self-disciplined person alone is not enough if you are not willing to keep that momentum going.

It's the same with mastering your emotions. The intention to control and boost your EI skills to become a better leader alone is not enough.

You need to keep the ball rolling, which is why persistence is another important trait which you need to build as part of your character.

Your very success will depend upon your ability to persist even when the odds are not in your favour.

Setbacks will happen, wrenches will be thrown in your plan, and in the face of all that, you must persist with self-discipline to see you through.

Persistence can be a surprisingly rewarding emotion.

Each time that you force yourself to see a task through, the result is going to make you feel much happier and better about yourself.

As part of this ripple effect, that feeling is going to drive you to want to do more, to see just how far you can go if you only just persist on a task using willpower and self-discipline.

Even if you were to have bucket loads of self-discipline, if you're not willing to persist, the success which should be within your grasp is only going to slide further out of reach.

The way that you respond to the setbacks that you face will be the deciding factor about how ready you are to succeed in your life.

Setbacks have a way of messing with our emotions, making us feel discouraged, despondent, and even question why this is happening when you have put in the effort that you were supposed to. It makes you question whether you should give up.

A strong leader, however, knows that giving up is not an option.

Great leaders never give up—they simply strive to be better. This is the exact moment that you need to rise to the challenge, to pull in persistence and self-discipline together because it is not about how hard you fall, but it is your ability to get back up and dust yourself off that matters.

Shake it off and tell yourself you can still do this, and use the following keys to help you succeed:

- Starting Small - Again, it's not a race.

You don't need to decide you want to improve today and wake up determined to turn things around completely tomorrow.

It doesn't work like that. Change—big change, especially— needs time (this cannot be stressed enough).

The desire to change is a great start, but instead of waking up the next day wanting to do it all, start small and pick one thing that you want to focus on changing first. It can do wonders to prevent you from feeling overwhelmed.

- Be Solution-Oriented - The key to winning at self-discipline and persistence is to focus on the solution instead of the problem.

Finding a solution should take priority and remind yourself that setbacks are only temporary. In fact, each time you face an unexpected setback, train your mind to think about what solution you need right now, which will help you overcome this.

Solutions will keep you persisting and moving forward, using self-discipline as a springboard for that determination to let nothing deter you.

- Think About What You Want to Be Done Differently - You know you want to change.

The question is, what do you want to change?

It's important to be specific with the details, as being vague is going to make it hard for you to have something concrete to focus on.

If you say you want to improve your leadership abilities, what specifically about your leadership style do you think needs work?

- See Setbacks as A Benefit - This is the last thing you would probably expect, but here is why it works.

If you think about the past challenges and setbacks that you faced which you managed to overcome eventually anyway, instead of looking at the downside, consider the takeaway lessons each setback left you with.

Did it make you a much stronger person?

Did it turn out to be a blessing in disguise?

Did it add something of value to your life in a way you might not otherwise have had the opportunity of experiencing?

If you can train yourself to view each setback as a gift instead of a demotivating element, you will do wonders to transform your persistence and levels of self-discipline.

- Get Rid of Bad Habits - It's very, very important that you rid yourself of all the bad habits that have been holding you back all this time.

This is why self-discipline is such a crucial trait to have because, without it, it can become very easy to fall by the wayside and continually find reasons why you cannot get things done.

Always ask yourself if you are spending your time in the best possible way for your benefit before you decide on a course of action.

- There's Never Going to Be A "Right" Time - If you're always waiting for the right time to start, you're going to be waiting forever.

The right time is what you make of it, and it is up to you how you choose to handle yourself from now on.

Time is precious, and every moment you have needs to count for something, that's what a good leader does.

- Get Yourself a Mentor - Having a role model that you can look up to and focus on can do a lot for your self-disciplinary intentions, and it serves as living proof that sticking to the path and seeing it through all the way to the end does work—that self-discipline works.

A mentor is also someone who's had more experience, which is something you're going to be able to benefit from.

Get yourself a mentor to give you advice when you struggle, guide you when obstacles have you stumped for a solution, and even give you feedback about how you've been doing so far.

In this case, a mentor can prove to be a valuable asset.

Key Takeaway Points

- Too much empathy can be a bad thing when it starts to affect you more than it should. Be careful not to let it affect you to a point where it starts draining you of your energy levels and severely affecting your emotions.

- Stress can affect those as young as kids, and stress knows no age limitations. Stress is not restricted to one specific gender alone, as both men and women can feel equal amounts of stress.

- Chronic stress is bad for you because over time, the weight of this negative emotion is going to be debilitating both mentally and physically.

- Take care of yourself first—only then will you be able to take care of your stress levels, as well as your physical and emotional wellbeing.

- Charisma and self-discipline are the two other traits you need to help you relate to others and keep your emotions in check.

- Charisma and charm are personality traits that you can create for yourself, and that is one of the many secrets and techniques successful people possess.

- Self-discipline is something that takes persistence and practice, not an accomplishment that can be done overnight. Practice it every day until you perfect it, no matter how long it takes.

- Persistence can be a surprisingly rewarding emotion.

EMOTIONAL INTELLIGENCE FOR LEADERSHIP

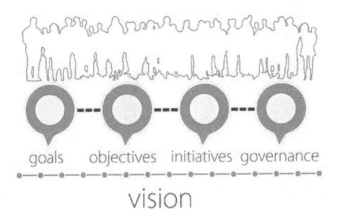

goals   objectives   initiatives governance

vision

In this chapter, we shall take a detailed look at these key elements and see how they can improve the leader's ability to lead well. This chapter will highlight leadership skills from an emotional perspective — their benefits and how these abilities can help leaders become more effective.

Self-Awareness

Self-awareness is our ability to accurately identify his or her weaknesses, strengths, emotions, and subsequent responses. Being self-aware requires an in-depth awareness of how your emotions influence your thoughts and actions. This is the basis upon which any meaningful changes can be internalized. Without practicing self-awareness, it is almost impossible for anyone (leader or not) to making lasting changes to their lives or careers.

Leaders who don't have a strong sense of self-awareness are often under a lot of stress both at home and at the workplace. They are practically at the mercy of their emotions. This is why the practice of self-awareness is the basis upon which every other skill, leadership ability, and other elements of emotional intelligence are built.

The practice of self-awareness should not be confused with being overly critical or judgmental. The goal of self-awareness is to recognize emotions in a non-judgmental attitude. It is not aimed at making you feel bad about your feelings. When you can calmly name your emotions by saying things like, "I am feeling sad at the moment," without thinking you are bad or weak for feeling that way, you are exercising self-awareness in the right direction.

Self-awareness is also known as meta-cognition – the knowledge of your cognitive processes. Instead of reacting to your emotions, meta-cognition simply puts you in the observation mode where you can note what is causing you to feel the way you do.

Benefits of Self-awareness

- Working on your strengths to speed up goal actualization.
- Recognizing and working with people who are strong in areas where you are weak. This will create a positive impact on your organization's output.

- Taking calculated risks with a clear awareness of your weaknesses.
- Makes negative feedback easy to handle.
- Using mistakes as opportunities for growth.
- Setting and maintaining healthy boundaries in line with your strengths and weaknesses.
- You are hardly taken unawares by your behavioral responses since you understand your emotions and know why you respond the way you do.

How to Improve Self-awareness

1. Get in the habit of identifying writing down your emotional triggers. A trigger could be a person, situation or a specific behavior. As you identify these triggers, write them down one after the other, including what you thought about them, how you felt, and your subsequent behavior or response. The more you can do this, the better you will be able to recognize patterns in your emotions and reactions. This will help you in self-regulation.

2. Mentally note how others react to the different ways in which you behave. Write down these reactions if possible. Study these reactions to find trends or patterns. If the general reaction to a certain behavior is positive or negative, that information will help you realize if it requires modifying or not.

3. Request honest feedback from your team. To make it easier for them, let them send in their feedback anonymously.

Self-Regulation

Identifying your emotions and why you respond to them the way you do is one thing, but it is quite another thing to control or regulate those responses. If you have identified that you easily snap at your subordinates angrily when they appear indecisive, that is a first important step. Through self-awareness, you have learned that indecision in others triggers you and makes you feel irritated, and you respond by snapping at them angrily. However, if you stop the process at knowing that weakness, you are still stuck in behavior that shows you lack emotional intelligence.

The next step requires that you become deliberate about managing the emotion or your response to the emotion. Let them out by using the methods earlier discussed so that they do not accumulate and explode in an uncontrollable outburst.

As a leader, if you allow your emotions to get in your way, it will deter you and your team from meeting deadlines and harmoniously working towards attaining your goals.

Do not confuse self-regulation to mean shutting off all negative emotions. Leaders are human beings, and as such have both positive and negative emotions. It is unhealthy to try and coerce yourself into feeling only positive emotions. The goal of practicing self-regulation should be to deliberately be in charge of your emotions and diffuse them effectively. It is not focused on picking out only feel-good emotions.

The following are a few examples of how leaders can demonstrate self-regulatory behaviors:

1. A leader or employee who remains calm and polite when a client is shouting down the roof and wrongly accusing them.

2. Not allowing emotions to get in the way when a request is turned down by superiors.

3. When a leader refrains from yelling at his or her direct reports due to their sluggish performance.

4. When a leader under stressful situations intentionally delegates tasks to his or her subordinates to give him or her room to tackle their emotions.

Benefits of Self-regulation

- Causes you to become flexible and adaptable to change.
- Reduces your chances of embarrassment due to irrational behaviors.
- You are looked upon as dependable and rationally stable.
- You think through before taking action.
- Helps you to be proactive about your emotional tendencies.

How to Improve Self-regulation

1. Be open to change. Being rigid can cause you serious emotional hurts. Being flexible will make you adapt to changing situations.

2. Understand that you will make mistakes and own up when you do. Accept responsibility for your emotions and how you respond or behave. That is the easiest way to effect corrections. Don't shift the blame to someone else, "He made me so mad!" No, he didn't. You let yourself become so mad.

3. Always try to physically or mentally distance yourself from your emotional triggers. Even a few brief moments spent away from stressful situations can have a huge impact on your practice of self-regulation. Remember to consciously breathe as you distance yourself from those situations.

4. Ask yourself what the consequences of your behavior or response would be. In the brief moment that exists between the trigger and your response, do a quick mental assessment of what your best move will be given the situation at hand.

I have compiled below some quick exercises that are geared toward helping you improve your ability to self-regulate.

1. No matter how busy your schedule is, find time daily to laugh heartily.

2. Practice positive affirmations to quieten your inner chatter.

3. Exercise regularly.

4. Sleep for about 7 to 8 hours daily.

5. Drink more water; reduce alcohol consumption.

6. Use self-hypnosis to reduce stress level.

7. Practice mindfulness meditation.

8. Do not neglect family and social life. Find a balance between work and other aspects of your life.

9. Spend time every once in a while to reflect on your behaviors.

Self-Motivation

Self-motivation is being enthusiastic about your goals and vision due to your inner drive. Self-motivated leaders are not primarily focused on money, status or power. This inner drive helps them set their sights beyond any seeming obstacle and keeps them fixated and persistent on their goals.

Self-motivated leaders can stifle all the external and internal noises and focus on the task at hand. Emotions don't derail or distract them. They always keep the bigger picture in perspective irrespective of the bad behavior or poor performances of their team. They don't lose their cool and throw the baby out with the bathwater! They can sift through emotional noise to pick out the important things.

Leaders can leverage self-motivation to increase personal and team performance. They use negative emotions such as worry to fuel their ingenuity instead of allowing it to dim their focus. For example, rather than acting irrationally and thinking, "I can't possibly meet this deadline. I am finished!" an emotionally intelligent leader will use that same emotion to think along the lines of, "I must do everything in my power to meet this deadline. I am willing to think out of the box and get suggestions on how best and quickly to meet this deadline."

Benefits of Self-Motivation

- Significantly cuts down indecisiveness and procrastination.
- It significantly boosts the self-confidence of the leader.
- It improves self-discipline.
- Creates the willingness to stick to visions and goals.
- Makes you optimistic about life in general, including your work and team in particular. This helps you become more open to welcome new ideas that will translate into progress for you and your team.
- Negative situations do not easily weigh you down. Your motivation level is usually high regardless of the challenging situation.
- Helps you to see and approach problems as challenges.
- Keeps you unflustered by seemingly insurmountable challenges.

How to Improve Self-motivation

1. Find out what your purpose is for your career and your team.

2. After discovering your purpose, you must become completely engrossed in the idea of your purpose. Burn it

into your mind as your vision. Let it be the driving force that propels you to lead your team.

3. Be very realistic when setting your goals. Remember to always break them down into baby steps so that you are not overwhelmed by their enormity.

4. Help others who need motivation. By supporting others morally, you are keeping your motivation alive.

5. Keep track of your team performances and measure them against your goals. This will help you to know when your team is deviating from your goals and if they are making significant progress toward your goal.

6. Give yourself rewards (no matter how small) for every milestone you reach along the way to your goal. You can extend this gesture to your team as well to keep their motivation up. Recognize even the slightest of improvement and effort they put into their work.

7. Remain optimistic in the face of setbacks. Understand that there will definitely be some setbacks along your path as you pursue your vision. Don't let them get to you. You will, somehow, find a way to bounce back from setbacks if you remain optimistic.

8. Create momentum and don't let it slow down. If you cannot increase your team's momentum, ensure you maintain it. For example, if you and your team start by collectively sending 30 marketing email campaigns per

day, do your best to figure out ways to increase or maintain that tempo.

9. Believe in your vision and take steps toward achieving them even if it means making mistakes along the way. Mistakes only go to prove that you are making decisions and also making progress.

10. Shun comparison. Other leaders have their own purposes for doing what they do which you may not know anything about. Moreover, what they are reaching for may be totally different from what you set out to achieve. So, focus on yourself and your team.

11. Learn new skills and also encourage your team to do things differently. Changing routines every once in a while will reduce the chances of getting bored, derailed, and losing your focus.

12. When faced with challenging situations, try to shift your focus to the bright side of the situation. Training your mind to seek out the good in a seemingly bad situation will further help you to keep your motivation up.

13. Keep yourself surrounded by people and things that motivate and inspire you.

14. Don't neglect the need for breaks. Continuous grinds can lead to burnout. Rest and reaction are necessary to recharge yourself and your team.

Empathy

Empathy means the ability to recognize and understand the feelings of others. For a leader to be empathic, he or she must, first of all, develop the ability to accurately recognize emotions in others. This means that an emotionally intelligent leader can temporarily set aside his or her own point of view so that they can step into the shoes of the person they are interacting with. This will help the leader determine, without judgment, what is causing the other person's behavior.

Pretending to be empathic will not elicit the same response that genuine empathy would. Developing empathy requires sincerity of purpose and a willingness to truly connect with the other person.

Empathic leaders are very sensitive to detect shifts in the moods of the people they work with. Words need to be spoken for the leader to know that the other person is having some emotional issues. This is because empathic leaders are well attuned to reading non-verbal cues.

Benefits of Empathy

- It increases your ability to be compassionate and understand people's plight.
- It creates a stronger bond within the team.
- It enables you to deliver constructive feedback without damaging the morale of your team.
- It improves the quality of your communication with others.

- It helps you to connect genuinely with your team on a deeper level. This improves the quality of your relationship with them.

How to Improve Empathy

1. Engage in continuous learning and reading to broaden your horizon. The more diverse the topic you learn, the more you will gain an understanding about other people's perspective.

2. Regularly challenge your beliefs, prejudices, biases, and preconceived ideas. The more you clear the clutter that can constitute as barriers from your minds, the easier it will be to connect with others. However, do not lose sight of your authenticity in the process.

3. Avoid rushing into conclusions. Withhold judgment and being critical until you get all the facts of the matter. Give people the benefit of the doubt.

4. Listen attentively when your team member or other people are speaking with you. Do not focus on planning your response or interrupt them while they are speaking. Hold your attention riveted on them and be fully present with them. Try to understand their perspective as you listen.

5. You share some things in common with the people you interact with. Let your mind focus on those similarities instead of the differences.

6. Try to gauge the feelings and moods of the people you interact with without losing focus on the interaction. If you are just starting to improve your empathy level, don't appear too desperate to connect with the other person. Avoid making it obvious that you are gauging their feelings.

Social Skills

Your ability to manage the emotions of others as well as influence them is referred to as social skills. This is where your power to positively influence your team as a leader comes into play. Nevertheless, it is important to mention at this point that positively influencing your team becomes a lot easier if you improve your social skills.

First, you must be able to successfully manage your emotions as a leader before attempting to manage those of others. Empathy is also a key element that can hardly be separated from social skills. A combination of these key elements will ensure that you can effectively influence your team positively.

Setting the tone for interacting with others becomes easier if you can improve your social skills. When interacting with people who are emotionally down, you can combine empathy with social skills to connect deeply with them so that you can gradually shift their perspective to a more beneficial one. In other words, your team and others who interact with you stand to gain emotional benefits from you as a leader. This will eventually increase their level of trust and confidence in you and also improve the quality of the relationship you have with your them.

Improving your social skills doesn't mean you have to please everyone on your team or everyone you come across. You do not have to pretend to be who you are not. Social skills also mean developing your assertive muscles so that you can remain true to your convictions, truths, and values.

Benefits of Social Skills

- Improves your chances of building a strong rapport with your team.
- Helps you to build a strong social capital and to attract like-minded people to yourself.
- Boosts your self-esteem as you can interact confidently with almost anyone. You will be more comfortable interacting even with strangers and can effectively communicate even in large groups.
- Helps you to quickly manage conflict that is bound to occur among team members.
- Open you up to more opportunities either on a personal or professional level.

How to Improve Social Skills

1. Put your best foot forward when interacting with people. It doesn't matter if you are interacting with superiors or subordinates, be polite and demonstrate good manners. Show appreciation and gratitude.

2. Keep your questions open-ended when interacting with your team. This will encourage them to offer useful suggestions and insights. When you ask questions that limit their responses to either yes or no, you cut yourself off from potentially productive ideas that can move you and your team towards your goals.

3. Start conversations no matter how awkward or difficult they may be. The more you engage with your people, the better you get to know them, and the easier it will be to engage even in the toughest of conversations.

4. Be generous as well as honest about compliments and praises. It gives people a warm sense of welcome and you come across as friendly.

5. Develop a genuine interest in what matters most to your team.

6. Build a strong rapport with your team by learning how to mirror body language.

HOW TO BECOME A LEADER

When we started on this journey, we did mention in the introductory section that this book is for two sets of individuals: leaders and potential leaders.

If you are a leader already, there are lessons you can gain from this chapter as well. Unlike some other materials that may focus on how to help you become a leader, this chapter entails details on how you can develop into a leader using EQ techniques.

This means that you wouldn't need to take on another foundational EQ lesson because it is part of the leadership class you will be getting now. The idea of being a leader over others is always very glamorous in people's minds because we all love the thrill of having people under our command or influencing them.

But leadership is not an idea you can incorporate just because you want it. You will be responsible for people, and without preparation for it, there will be problems.

It is excellent that you desire a leadership role, but the real question is, are you ready to handle it? Can you take on the burden of vision for a group? There are so many facets to that idea, which is the reason why this chapter is so crucial.

Now you may be a leader already, and you are not getting it right because you didn't get proper training. You also don't have a good foundation. Think of this chapter as another opportunity for you to get it right.

Learn from Leaders You Admire

There are leaders around you who are excelling in their roles; those leaders should be an inspiration to you as you take on this path. Some people give up midway into the leadership experience because they didn't get the time to understudy an accomplished leader, so they had no one to look up to at the time.

To avoid the pitfall of giving up too quickly, you need to seek out the leaders you admire. Get to learn some of the tenants of leadership directly from someone who is living the dream.

This leader could be someone in your family, your place of work, or somewhere else, but it has to be someone accessible. Your role with this first step is to observe them, watch how they relate with their followers, and see how they take on decision-making processes. If the leader you admire works in the same organization as you, it might be an opportunity for you to approach them for a mentorship opportunity.

Too many people strive to become leaders without adequate training; hence, the reason they don't turn out to be great leaders. But you can do better, which is why the first step entails you reaching out to someone already doing excellently what you desire to do.

Success with every aspect of life leaves clues. If you observe a person's pattern and blend it in with your authentic self, you will surely become a leader. However, you must be mindful while implementing this step, so you don't end up losing yourself in the process.

All you should do is observe and pick up on inspiring traits you can develop that will help you achieve your leadership goal.

Build Requisite Skills for the Position

It is excellent that you want to be a leader, but do you have the skills needed for the job? No one will make you a leader because you desire it when others are more competent than you. So while studying leaders you admire, carry out some research on the position you want to take on as a leader. Ask relevant questions such as: What can I do to get there? What qualifications do I need? What are the skillsets required for the position? How long will it take for me to learn them? Where can I begin? Is it possible to learn online?

When you get your answers, be proactive with implementing them. Get to know the ones you've done already and the ones you will need to develop. Skills are valuable all over the world, but something is better than the skills you possess at the moment, and that is additional skills.

When you join an organization, you are brought in based on the skills you possess. But after a while, if you don't upgrade those skills, you will not be able to aspire to leadership. Go over, and beyond what everyone else can do. This is what makes you exceptional! Become extremely good at acquiring new skills that people within the team come to you for help because you are always ahead.

However, be excited about learning these new skills, or else you will not be motivated to do it. As a potential leader, you must avoid mediocrity and stick with excellence. By excellence, we mean being excited about the idea of learning and putting in the required amount of time into it.

Find joy in what you do, and you will do it even better!

Be a Team Player

Leadership is all about working closely with a team or a group of people to achieve a specific goal. The purpose of administration is to create a synergy between people. Such synergy will harness all of their strengths for the benefit of the higher goal.

This means that, for you to become a leader, you must know how to work with a team (be a team player). Of course, there are varying types of leadership, and dictatorship is one of them, but this isn't a great form of leadership.

Even if within your current organization, you have a dictator, please realize that there is a better leadership model that works, and it entails working closely with a team. You may not be a leader in an official capacity yet, but you can provide an excellent example while preparing for your role by being a team player.

Even when you've got a fantastic idea, don't go solo with it, take your team with you on the ride and share the win or victory. Leaders leave no one behind, so regardless of the role they all play on the group, it is your responsibility to carry everyone along.

Everyone will achieve more together, and the group will also need a strong leader who can harness the potentials of each one in the group. For you to know the abilities of those in your team, you will need to become an emotional leader who uses emotional intelligence.

Practice this step wherever you are now. Start learning how to work with people and develop a culture of teamwork.

Take Up Responsibilities

Leadership is about responsibilities! So yes, the prestige of the position and the respect it brings are attractive, but remember that you will be required to do more and take on more and more responsibilities. In your workplace, if you want to become a leader or get that promotion you've desired for a long time, do more! While everyone else does only paid hours and leaves at the exact time they have to go, put in some extra effort.

See your manager, superior, or boss and indicate that you're interested in doing more for the organization. This move will set you apart from others who are also interested in the leadership role.

Within your department, be sure to always give your whole. Be the man or woman who is committed to getting the job done. Taking on more responsibilities may help you get you the role you desire. This move sends a strong message to your superiors that you are a top choice for a leadership role. It will not be easy for you to take on more in addition to what you already do. But you must remember that you are training for leadership, and if you want to be the best at it, you must put in the work.

When you take on more responsibilities, you do not only get the attention of the bosses; you also get the attention and respect of your peers. Interestingly, you will become very proficient in multiple tasks because of this dedication. While others try to avoid responsibilities, be excited about it, and seize those opportunities to add value to yourself. When it is time to choose the head of the team, you will be the best candidate for the job.

Share Your Vision and Ideas

The fact that you desire leadership means you have a desire in your heart, and you want things better than they are now. Bravo! So what you need to do is nurture that vision. Then share it with others on a similar path as you.

Leaders are known to be outspoken people who share ideas, even if such views don't receive implementation. But by sharing, they become known as individuals who are intelligent and capable of leading excellently. Wherever you are now is your opportunity to practice for your leadership role. Don't be shy or afraid to put your hand up and share your ideas when people search for solutions in a gathering.

When you become outspoken, it will be easy for you to stand out from the crowd. People will always reach out to you when they need advice or ideas to solve a problem. More importantly, you can rise above the process of poor decision making caused by groupthink.

The concept of groupthink exists in every gathering, organization, or family. Groupthink refers to the practice of people within a group making irrational decisions because they strive for a consensus. Now when there is a challenge in a group, most people may have a unique solution. But because they don't share their ideas, they settle for what the majority says.

But if you are going to become a leader, you must learn how to rise above the majority (especially if you know you have a better solution) and speak out. A true leader is not afraid to speak out because they realize that for their vision to become a reality, it has to be shared.

All of these efforts culminate in making you an exceptional leader with high EQ.

Be Emotionally Available for Others

People always surround leaders because they are in a position to change situations, make decisive decisions, and influence circumstances. However, you are used to being alone and doing things your way; hence, the reason you don't know how to be emotionally available for others.

Now is the time to develop being emotionally available because you will need it to become a leader. Whenever it is election season in any country, you will observe that a candidate with an emotional connection to people gets a favorable lead. The reason for this occurrence during the election period is because everyone (even kids) wants a leader that cares. We all want to know that when we are in a problematic situation, we can go to our leader for solutions and emotional comfort.

So you must work on your emotional availability. The best way to do that is to start thinking of others. Start at home and then take it to the office and everywhere else.

Emotional availability is about the little things like asking someone how their day was, being there for them when they are down, and generally being a great support system.

If you work with a team, be known as the one who stands in when someone is sick or the friend they can count on when there is a crisis. Some people say, "It is lonely at the top," because leaders have to be there for everyone, but no one is there for them. But that statement is not entirely true. A leader who is known for emotional availability will always have a real support system.

Take on Consistent Self-Development

To become a leader, you must be passionate about self-development. You want to lead, influence, and inspire people, but you cannot give what you don't have. So while aspiring for leadership, use every opportunity you have to add more value to yourself. Develop new skills, read good books, take on new courses, and generally do more to become better.

If you are in a group with people who are hoping for a promotion or leadership position, it might be a mild competition. But you should know that the organization will only settle for the person they believe is being intentional about self-development.

What you knew in the past brought you this far, but what you dedicate yourself to understanding now will determine the success of your leadership aspirations. The reason some people never get more leadership roles or opportunities is that they stick to information about their sector alone. Such people have the same repeated routine! They don't read anything new, they don't take on new roles, and they are generally passive within the organization.

However, when you take self-development seriously those around you will notice the changes self-development adds to your life. So when it is time to decide on a leader for a new sector, you will top the list.

Don't take self-development lightly. In this technological age, you can gain access to information of any kind. Instead of always going to your boss to ask a question, try to find answers through consistent learning.

Use search engines, YouTube, and social media intentionally for learning. Don't wait until you get your letter for a leadership role before taking self-development steps. This idea should be something that you do daily and consistently; it never ends! Even when you do become a leader, you shouldn't stop upgrading yourself. Read more, share what you learned with a friend, and keep adding value to your leadership. When you become passionate about self-development, like you are right now about EQ, you will also propel those you follow to do the same.

Use Feedback and Criticism to Grow

If you don't like criticism, then you will need to work on yourself. As a leader, you will deal with criticism a lot (maybe even more than you expect). Criticisms aimed at leaders are not personal attacks (when done right), so you must learn to live beyond the hurtful words and pick the message of the critic.

Wherever you are now, there might be one or two people who criticize your work, ideas, and the way you handle your job. Instead of getting upset over what someone said, filter the comment, take the corrective action, and let the rest go.

Feedback is also another aspect of leadership you must prepare for as it helps you get information on the decisions you made. Feedback also lets you know if your decisions helped your team achieve their goals or not. Always intentionally ask for feedback from people you do things for because it is the only way through which you can get a direct response/rating on your performance.

If you are already a leader and you haven't been asking for feedback, now is a good time to do that. If you are a potential leader, start asking for feedback in your family, workplace and everywhere else you do something for someone or a group of people.

Now even when you know you've got a fantastic job, don't always expect positive feedback. Be open-minded towards what will be said and use it as a tool to get better. You must start getting used to it now before taking on a leadership role.

As regards criticism, allow it to get to your head where you can analyze and break it down to get details you can use to make the system better. But don't allow it get to your heart or else you will become angry and upset. You will feel hurt when you believe that you are doing an excellent job.

Treat People with Respect

Respect is reciprocal: for you to get it, you must give it! So to be a great leader, you must show respect to the people you lead because they come first. Be courteous and polite to them just as you would want them to be towards you.

A lot of things change as an individual climbs the leadership ladder. There is increased boldness and confidence with better decision-making skills because now the leader has gained a lot of insight through experience.

But what should never change for you is the respect you give to those who follow you. A respectful leader uses the words "please," "I'm sorry," and "thank you" a lot. This leader is mindful of boundaries placed by followers and respects them.

If you are not a leader in any capacity yet, try practicing respect for others with the people around you, especially those you may be superior to (in terms of position). If you are a parent, show some respect for your kids and their friends. If you are on a bus, respect the driver! If you go to a restaurant to eat, also show some respect for the waiter.

The fact that you are a leader or you are going to be one doesn't mean that you cannot come down from your exalted position. Show respect for those you think are below your rank. Respect shown to those who follow you will be an indication of how connected you are to them and that it isn't all about you!

Be True to Yourself

Above all, you must stay true to yourself!

Some people become excessively desirous of leadership roles that when they do get it, they immerse themselves and lose their essence. Such persons spend time studying other great leaders and try to duplicate their styles and methods. But there can only be one great leader who has their form and leadership ability. You can admire a leader and emulate him/her but retain your essence by being true to yourself. Do things the way you want to do them and let people value your uniqueness.

A lot of times, some people worry about acceptance; hence, the reason they try to be like someone else. When you become a leader, the perception of others will matter to you, but it shouldn't rule over you.

Don't strive to be liked. Instead, desire respect.

A leader who wants likeness will become a people pleaser. They will never be able to take a stand for something if everyone else doesn't support their decision.

This desire for popular support is a significant trait of weak leadership! Don't try to copy another leader because you assume those you lead wouldn't like your style. Of course, there will be improvements, but first, begin on an authentic note.

When you are inconsistent by trying to copy various successful leaders, those you lead will notice that trait and take advantage of you. More so, you will lose the respect of your followers, subordinates, and employees. We all love originality, so be a unique person, and people will love and respect you for being real.

It is possible that after reading through this book, you will be able to raise others as leaders as well using the ideas shared thus far. For those who are already leaders, you know the best way to solidify the learning process is to practice and keep at it until it becomes a part of you. More so, you should know that leadership is a process. It is a journey you begin, but it never ends because when you become a leader. You continue to remain passionate about people.

That passion will propel you always to lead wherever you find yourself. Be a leader that inspires and influences others positively. Be an emotional leader who creates a firm connection with others such that they are free to become vulnerable around you.

Now you know the traits of a great leader. It is time to take on an aspect of leadership that has been mentioned repeatedly in this book. Can you tell what we are taking on next?

Are you enjoying this book? It would mean a lot to me having a short review. Thank you!

POSITIVE APPROACH

You see, this elf knew how to live. He understood long ago that there must be joy in life. Only joy. However, it does not happen just like that. It must be let into your life. It is everywhere around, this joy, but many people are deprived of it because they are afraid to let it into life. And, of course, the longer people live without joy, the more it scares them, and even more, they try not to let it close, and then it suddenly turns out that there was no joy in their life at all.

A positive approach is not at all the same as blind optimism and pink glasses. Its essence in the name "positive" comes with a deeper meaning that is, "what is available". Here, you can recall the famous glass.

A pessimist sees a glass half empty. An optimist, contrary to the well-known statement, will notice that there is an opportunity to fill as much as half a glass! But a proponent of a positive approach will note that the glass is half full. What we call a positive approach is called "rational optimism"; reliance on what is good that is already in place, rather than on what is good in the future.

We do not offer to put on "pink glasses" immediately and think only about the good. People who are always positive can lose valuable information and poorly analyze possible mistakes ("But stop it, it will work out!"). Such an over positive approach is also irrational.

However, the positive train of thought is often less familiar to us. Meanwhile, "certain features of leadership behavior are associated with it. In particular, the desire to find favorable opportunities and overcome obstacles to achieving the goal, as well as sincere faith in people and a tendency to always hope for the best. People who are optimistic about things are able to work more productively than pessimists. They have a higher life expectancy. Moreover, optimism contributes to a general sense of well-being, and this, in turn, helps leaders restore their potential, withstand the trials and overcome the frustrations inevitably present in their work".

Some researchers argue that optimism or pessimism is an inherent trait. However, we are closer to the approach of Martin Seligman, the founder of positive psychology, who uses the term "learned optimism", bearing in mind that if you are more prone to a negative assessment of events, you can retrain yourself. It is this way of thinking that we offer you to master. A positive approach may include the use of the ABC scheme, when instead of negative thoughts, you prefer to use positive ones, reframing, as well as constructive feedback to yourself, relying on your own resources and strengths, the ability to show off and the ability to "turn on" well.

Constructive Feedback to Yourself

What do we say to ourselves if something doesn't work out for us or it doesn't work out in the best way? "Well, I'm a fool!", "Damn, again, I did everything wrong." or "Well, I ruined everything." Why do we need such a way to give feedback to ourselves? This one is just a completely emotional reaction in the sense that useful information in these statements is completely absent. In some cases, we take a step further and analyze our mistakes. "It was not necessary to do this and that, then everything would be better." More valuable information? Honestly, not much. If the situation is unique in its kind and you are sure that you will never find yourself in such a situation again, you can sprinkle ash on your head and analyze nothing. If the situation can happen at least with some degree of probability, the information that you really need is what you need to do next time in order to achieve the desired result.

Such information consists of two parts.

1. What actions will I repeat next time?

Pay attention to the word "repeat." That is, were my actions this time effective and successful (in terms of achieving the desired result)?

2. What else will I do? What will I do differently?

Please note "what I will do," and not "what I will not do anymore." You may be horrified now, but we will not need to analyze errors. At all. All our lives, we have been taught to look for mistakes.

Instead of the wrong actions, we need to find a picture of the right actions: what we will do instead. Remember translating a problem into a goal? The same principle works here: we are of little interest in what was wrong in our actions in the past; we are interested in what to do better next time.

That is, analyzing all the actions that we performed. We sort them into two groups: "Effectively, next time I will do the same" and "Next time I will do it differently" (instead of the standard "right / wrong" analysis).

Assignment

"Constructive feedback"

Imagine a situation: I arrived to negotiate with a client, being late for 15 minutes due to traffic jams. I go into his office and see the director in a jacket and with a tie tightened, while I arrived in jeans and a light blouse because it seemed to me that they had a very free corporate culture. I politely greeted and, in spite of the horror of how different our uniforms were, smiled sincerely. It turned out that I had forgotten business cards and a notebook to record the results of negotiations.

I asked a question I prepared, but the client did not answer it and said, "But tell me better about yourself." I started quite cheerfully to tell him about our company, and then he asked, "What do you know about us?" And when he asked this, I was horrified to remember that I had forgotten to look at their site. After answering a few general phrases, I repeated the question that I asked him at the very beginning. This time, he answered something, then scratched his head and said, "It seems to me that you don't understand this at all." I indignantly answered, "How do you know what I understand and what not?!" Then he said that it was too expensive, and we started talking about discounts. Then a bunch of people bursts into the office, and he said to me, "Sorry, my meeting is starting." And he began to talk with his people. I politely said goodbye and left.

Now, review the text again and write down all the effective actions that I have done. After that, write what you recommend the heroine to do differently next time. Not the mistakes she made! And what should she do differently in the next negotiations with the client?

Secondly, remember the recent work situation in which you are not very happy with your behavior. Analyze what goal you wanted to achieve, what your actions were effective in terms of achieving this goal, and what you could do more or differently next time.

The optimism researcher, Martin Seligman, the author of the term "learned optimism" or "rational optimism" has identified three pillars of pessimism:

- Generalization ("I never succeed at all");

- Immutability ("I have never succeeded and will never succeed");

- Self-incrimination ("and only I am to blame for all this").

Constructive feedback to oneself helps to "get around" these three pillars and give a clear and objective assessment of the situation. You should know, it is the assessment that causes us emotions. Describe as much as possible those actions that you did or could have done, instead of general recommendations like "You should be more confident."

More confident? Speak louder, or to speak more assertively, or to interrupt the interlocutor, or to poke a finger at him more smartly? Which of these?

Reliance on your Strengths

Pay attention to the statistics of successful people. They are not blind optimists, evaluating themselves extremely positively. However, compared with the average figures, they think more positively.

There is another limitation of society which prevents us from thinking and speaking positively about ourselves, "Bragging is not good." The society encourages a critical attitude towards oneself and a constant desire for improvement. And that's good because it helps us move forward. However, it is difficult to move forward without having anything behind, without any resources.

Most educational systems teach you how to deal with defeat. At school, children are warned that they may have difficulty getting a job, even if they have a diploma. They try to prepare them at home for the idea that most marriages end in divorce and that most of the partners in life will eventually disappoint you.

Insurance companies support general pessimism. Their motto: there are many chances that you will have an accident, fire, or flood, so be prudent, be safe. The media reminds from morning to evening that people around the world are defenseless. Listen to the fortune-tellers, everyone is talking about the Apocalypse or war.

Worldwide defeat, local defeat, personal defeat; only those who talk about a bleak future are heard. Which prophet dares to declare that in the future everything will be better and better? But on an individual level, who dares to teach children at school what to do, having received an Oscar for the best role? How to respond after winning a world tour? What if your small business has grown into an international corporation?

When victory comes, a person is deprived of guidance, and often, he is so stunned that he quickly organizes his own defeat in order to find himself in the familiar "normal" environment".

The Brag Mission

Every day, write down what you did well and successfully today. What did you do? What made you happy?

We do not call to constantly be in a positive mood. Fear, anger, and sadness are also useful emotions and, allowing only positive emotions in our lives, we lose a lot of information and may miss something important. At the same time, when we are positive, it is much more difficult to be upset or lose our temper. Thus, a positive approach creates solid support for us under our feet and a kind of protection against the excessive influence of unpleasant events and emotions on us.

Leadership Recovery

The extremely stressful nature of the work of leaders leads to a special form of stress; managerial stress. Here are just a few factors that contribute to this:

- The manager has the burden of responsibility for the fate of the organization.

- The leader sets, as a rule, ambitious goals and strives to achieve results at all costs.

- Managers are constantly considering risks and negative options for the development of the situation; so they think a lot about the "worst" that can happen.

- The behavior of the leader is constantly observed and evaluated by others, so he has to be especially careful in controlling his behavior and his emotions.

The constant burden of responsibility and the need to make important decisions in a short time leads to fatigue of the leader. Fatigue is not so much physical as psychological. Many managers are faced with what is called "impostor syndrome" when the leader thinks, "Am I as good as everyone thinks of me?" Psychological fatigue leads to the fact that both self-esteem and the emotional state of the leader become unstable.

What does "restoring leadership potential" mean? Here we talk about three pillars: activity of consciousness, optimism, and empathy. The activity of consciousness, in fact, is almost the same as awareness, and optimism is the same as the positive approach. Thus, you are already familiar with all three pillars of restoring leadership potential.

In summary, there are several fundamental principles in managing your emotions. This is taking responsibility for your emotional state on yourself, the principle of accepting your emotions, and the principle of goal-setting. We all know a large number of ways to control emotions. They do not always work, because we do not know how to recognize our emotions. In addition, it is difficult to understand a large variety of techniques.

The main thing that is required to control your emotions is the awareness and acceptance of the fact that "I" alone am responsible for my emotional state. "I" choose how to feel at a given moment in time, and "I" feel just that.

To manage your emotions, it is important to reformulate your inhibitions on feeling any particular emotions and find a way to admit that "I" can experience different emotional states, even those that I used to consider "bad". Only then is it possible to control (rather than suppress) emotions.

The way in which emotions are managed and how it will act depends on the goal of interaction we set for ourselves and what result we want to get. Depending on this, the means of achieving the goal are selected. We structured the various techniques into a "quadrant for controlling our emotions." Under the control of emotions, we understand two processes: a decrease in the intensity of "negative" emotion and inducing or enhancing a "positive" emotion. In addition, managing emotions can be situational or strategic offline methods.

Among the short-term methods of controlling emotions, the most effective are bodily techniques (breathing techniques and physical activity). You can also record your emotions, pronounce them and restore communication with logic. If it's important for us to create an emotional state in private, then work on correcting them.

Strategic methods for managing emotions include the rational self-government scheme involving the reformulation of irrational beliefs, reframing, a positive approach, the development of goal-oriented thinking, and the restoration of leadership potential related to this scheme.

COPING WITH NEGATIVE EMOTIONS IN PEOPLE

To allow positive emotions to engulf you, you must make room for them in your life. The way that you do that is by clearing out and letting go of the negative emotions that are currently occupying space. Two strong emotions cannot live in the same space. One will overcome the other, and since it is human nature to veer towards the negative, there must be no room in your life for negative emotions.

The journey to positive empowerment begins now. Utilize the following tips every day, and watch your emotions transform from the inside:

- Just Breathe – This is all you need to start. Learn to slow yourself down whenever things feel like they might spiral out of control. Learning to take deep, measured breaths (something you will learn to do once you begin meditating) is an effective technique to release stress. Often underestimated and underutilized, repeated deep breathing in and out will help you relax and loosen the accumulated tension in your shoulders. You can physically feel yourself starting to unwind when you are forced to concentrate on nothing but the air that is moving through your body. With each breath, let go of a negative emotion. Think of it like a balloon, and with each breath you take, imagine the emotion floating away and leaving your body forever.

- Count It Out – Along with breathing, you should stop and count to 5 each time an emotion feels like it is going to overwhelm you. You can count to 5, 10, 15 or even 20 – any number that is going to calm you down and stop you from reacting impulsively. Release the negative emotions from your body with each count.

- Find Ways to Manage Your Stress – Everyone experiences stress. It just feels like a lot to handle when you're unable to properly cope with it because you've never made a conscious effort to do it before. Things are different now that you are actively working on improving your EQ. To do this, start by pinpointing all the triggers that give you stress and then look at what you can do to change that. Make a list (yes, make a list again) of anything that you feel is causing you stress, and work on eliminating those factors one by one. Stress is a negative emotion, and the only way to get rid of it is to tackle the problem from the root cause.

- Find Other Stress Relieving Outlets – Go for a walk, join a workout class you enjoy, go for a hike or a bike ride, find another outlet to relieve your stress instead of just letting your emotions boil and bubble underneath the surface as you try to bottle them up. Negative emotions have to go somewhere; why not multitask and release those emotions while simultaneously doing something that makes you feel good and happy (positive emotions)? If you're prone to being emotionally overwhelmed because you're stressed, it's time to start adopting relaxation techniques. Watch a comedy, indulge in your favorite TV shows, meditate or get together with a good friend so you can have a laugh.

- If You Need Help Ask – Working on eliminating all your negative emotions can be a challenging task for anyone to manage. It isn't an easy journey, and along the way, if you need help, don't be afraid to ask. Your commitment right now is to do what it takes to empower yourself, to fill your life with positivity, and asking for help is sometimes a necessary part of the process. Find someone that you would be comfortable talking to, someone you trust enough to rely on for help. Someone who could offer insight. Surround yourself with people who radiate positive energy – that's another good way to do it. The aura that you surround yourself with will eventually rub off on you.

- Remind Yourself That Bad Times Don't Last Forever – Stressful moments and sad times will come and go. Negative emotions do not last forever, although they certainly feel like they do. Whenever you find yourself in emotionally negative turmoil, remind yourself that the storm will pass. That you need to be strong. Over time, you will build up a tolerance and become tougher emotionally as you overcome each storm. The stronger and better you become, the more you will be filled with positive emotions as you slowly begin letting go of the negative ones.

- Positive Affirmations – Emotional times can be trying and put us through the wringer, and even though they don't last forever, it can be tough to remember that when you're going through it. Positive affirmations can be your best friend in this case. To start filling your life with positive empowerment, pick a couple of affirmations that empower you, and bring these affirmations with you whenever you go. Whenever negativity starts to get the best of you, whip out your affirmations and recite them over and over until your willpower feels strong enough to resist.

- Learning to Live in The Moment – Do you hold onto the past? Has not being able to accomplish something in the past stopped you from getting things done now because you can't let it go and your past failures keep infringing on your mind? Well, you need to stop. This is why you find it so difficult to let go of the negative emotions that weigh you down. Emotionally intelligent people do not hold onto the past; they live in the now. They focus on what they do today to shape the future that they want. They never hold onto the past, but they do learn from it and use those lessons as they make improvements for the future.

- Knowing When to Take Breaks – You may be ambitious and determined to work hard to improve your EQ, but you are not a robot or a machine that can work continuously without breaking down. People with high EQ are only human after all, and like you, they get tired. Yet, they still manage to get things done. How do they do it? By knowing when to take breaks. Emotionally intelligent people know how important taking occasional breaks are to recharge and refocus their minds. Feeling burned out and fatigued are not emotions which are positively empowering. Taking care of yourself is how you take the right step towards positive empowerment.

- Doesn't Let Your Emotions Distract You – How many times a day have you paused during a task because you got distracted by your emotions? Where negative feelings affect you so badly that you find it difficult to concentrate on the task at hand? Distractions are everywhere, but people with high EQ have mastered the art of regulating it and not letting their emotions distract them. They can completely remove distractions from their mind when there is something more important to focus on. In this case, positive empowerment. Remove all cause for temptation when you need to buckle down and get something done. Focusing on your emotions never does anyone any good – unless they are positive ones that motivate you toward success.

- Develop a System That Works for you – The reason you find it difficult to let go of negative emotions is because you haven't quite latched onto a system which works for you. Or the current system you have for regulating your emotions is not working well. In that case, it is time to think like an emotionally intelligent person and find a regulation system which works. It may take a couple of tries and practices before you find one that is just right.

How To Forgive Yourself And Forgive Others

We've all made mistakes. There is nobody who can go through life claiming they have never made a mistake since the day they were born. You need to learn to forgive yourself first before you can begin forgiving others. Accept your imperfections because you know those can always be improved.

Holding onto your past and repeatedly beating yourself up over it isn't going to change a thing because it has already happened. You're only human, and if you can accept other people for their flaws, you can certainly start accepting yourself too. Forgiving yourself is the simple part of the process; forgiving others is harder to wrap your head around. When someone has hurt us, especially if the hurt runs deep, it can be hard just to let go and let things go back to the way they were. Sometimes even the thought of the incident that happened is enough to bring all those feelings of hurt flooding right back into your mind, even if it is something that happened years ago.

How do you forgive the ones who have hurt you in the past?

- By Moving On – We know this is easier said than done, but it is the only way to begin learning to forgive. Realize that holding onto the past is only hurting you, not them. You are the one that is affected by it. Your emotions are the ones being tormented over the thought of it. Remind yourself that no matter how much you think about it, it is never going to change what happened. No amount of dwelling on the past ever will. The best thing for you is just to learn to let go, leave the past behind where it belongs and focus on looking ahead, the way emotionally intelligent people do.

- Never Go to Bed Angry – This is one exercise you should start adopting every night from now on. Make it a habit to never go to bed again with a negative emotion. It is simply not worth it. If there is nothing you can do to change it, then let it be. Why torture your emotions anymore over something that is never going to change? It's an unhealthy habit. Before you go to bed each night, do, watch or read something that lifts your spirits and puts you in a happy mood. Before you close your eyes and drift off to sleep, remind yourself of all the things you have to be grateful for.

- Accepting Responsibility – When confrontations and conflicts occur, it takes two people to rock the boat. While the other person may have had a bigger part to play in the falling out, you were also partially responsible on some level. Being someone with high EQ means that you need to use self-awareness to assess the situation objectively, to be able to see what mistakes you made and how you could have handled that better. From there, accept responsibility for the part that you played, and realize that both people involved were at fault to a certain degree.

- Choose to Be Kind Instead – Do you have the desire to be right all the time? Even if it means jeopardizing a relationship because you stubbornly refuse to let go of the need to be right? This could be one of the reasons why you're finding it hard to forgive. Instead of choosing to be right all the time, choose the emotionally intelligent way. Choose to be kind. Being a kind person is much better than being someone who is "right" all the time.

How To Free Yourself From Other People's Opinions And Judgment

Emotionally intelligent people are happier and more in control because not only do they not let their emotions control them, but they also don't let other people's opinions and judgments control them either. Caring too much about what other people think is how you get your emotions out of control. Have you ever been upset by what someone else said or thought about you? So, worked up that it was all you could obsess about for weeks or months? That's what caring too much about someone else's opinion will do to you.

To possess emotional intelligence means that you need to be confident enough to not care so much about what other people think. You need to free yourself from that chain which could hold you in an emotional prison. Ask yourself why you care so much about what this person thinks? What significance do they hold in your life? Do they matter enough to you to let it affect you this badly? If they play no major role in your life, why do you let their opinions matter?

The only opinions that you should care about are yours and those from the people who matter the most in your life – like your family and friends. The ones who genuinely care about you will only want what is best for you. They want you to be happy, and they will do everything that they can to be as supportive as possible.

Free yourself from this restrictive and unhealthy behavior by being true to yourself. Be who you are; don't try to be someone that you are not. You are the one that has to live your life. You are the one going through the obstacles, the challenges, the triumphs, and the successes. You are the one that picks yourself up when you fall – not the people who are passing negative judgment upon you. You only get one life to live, and you shouldn't be wasting any of it on comments which don't matter.

When someone else has a negative opinion of you, it is a reflection on them, not you. It is not a personal attack on you, especially if they are not someone of significance in your life. People are always quick to comment on the negative, and this is a trap you must not let yourself fall into. Brush it off, stand up tall and walk away, reminding yourself all the while that their opinion does not matter. Be confident and believe in yourself and know what you are worth. Treat the negative opinions and the judgment of others like they don't matter. Because they don't. It only matters if you let it matter.

CONCLUSION

This book has been a helpful tool to teach you about a plethora of topics but the main topics we have covered for you are, emotional intelligence, cognitive behavioral therapy, self-discipline and how to use this information in the real world. Emotional intelligence may be seen as a new area of study and as such it doesn't have all the studies that it needs to have completed, but there are enough studies to show that understanding your emotional intelligence will greatly benefit you in your professional life as well as your personal life. We've also been able to show you how understanding your intelligence quotient will be able to help you as well and the connection between your emotional intelligent quotient or EQ and your intelligence quotient or your IQ as well as showcasing each difference that they have as well so that you can see how they differ in import and how studies go back and forth on the subject.

Many businesses across the globe are looking for people who have a firm grasp on their emotional intelligence because many companies across the globe work as a team and it's not just about one person anymore. As a team you need to work together, and you need to be able to cohabitate together on many different projects. As such, no matter the situation that you're in or the different opinions that people have, you all need to be able to work together. This is where people who are in tune with their EQ comes in. Emotionally intelligent people make great leaders and they will be able to take each and every individual that's trying to work as a team and make sure that they are actually being turned into a fully functioning team which benefits the company much greater.

Emotionally intelligent people are good with management as well because they have the ability to perceive others emotions as well and they have the ability to keep their own emotions in check as well which helps in a professional setting because it sets a good example for the other employees and you can take them to the next level in their lives as well which means you are making a great difference.

There are also well known behavioral scientists who have made a lot of progress in the studies of emotional intelligence and how it affects us on a daily basis. This is something that really lets us see the new information that is available to us and how it can help us. Being able to use that information is also going to be able to help you when you're trying to get your emotional intelligence levels to the way you want them to be. Because emotional intelligence is a learned skill this means that you can raise it to the level that you want it to be and you can learn how to make yourself better. As we have mentioned in other chapters emotional intelligence is sought after, so much so that companies are now actively looking for people that have these skills and if they don't they make it apart of their hiring training, by the business world and any other career you could be thinking about getting into.

The business world is fraught with situations that you can get yourself into and you may not know what to do when you are trying to bring yourself up and advance yourself. When your trying to advance yourself and the world of business it's hard to understand what it is that you need to do and how it is you need to succeed. Having the ability to knowing your emotional intelligence level is going to be able to help you lead other people and inspire them to do great things as well. It is also going to help you be able to inspire yourself and take yourself to the next level where you thought you might not have been able to get to it's easy to take yourself to this next level and it's easy to understand how it is to get there once you understand what emotional intelligence is and why you should be concerned with it.

The intelligence quotient on the other hand is considered to be an ability that you are born with and as such there are debates as to whether or not this will work as emotional intelligence. Because this is such an important topic research is still being done to make the results and studies as accurate as possible. There are many that believe that you can always learn more and that the capacity for learning is vast as well.

Along with this because emotional intelligence can be learned you can always improve your skills and take them to the next level which will also help in your relationships and at work. People want to keep people on the staff that are constantly able to adapt and improve in their skills to make sure that they are always learning as much as they can.

This book is also going to teach you how you can use emotional intelligence to make yourself more aware. In life this is a very important skill that not many people are able to possess, and it is a necessary skill because this ability is going to give you a stronger sense of self, more confidence in your life and the ability to see things in a different way. In this life one of the gifts that we can be given is to know who we truly are and what we stand for. Being self-aware is also going to help you raise your emotional intelligence levels which is the main goal that we're trying to achieve here.

We've established that emotional intelligence has different levels and it can mean different things. We've taken the time to show you how each level is important to emotional intelligence as a whole. It's not just one thing that makes it up. It's a variety of different things coming together to make one thing whole. An example would be to think of yourself as a team. There are many things working in your body to make you who you are. Emotional intelligence is the same way. It's not just self-awareness or resilience that makes it up.

It's all different types of things that make it up and all of which need to be understood by you so that you can make sure that you're going into this knowing exactly what it is that you want to do and exactly how it is that you're going to do it. The same is true for cognitive behavioral therapy. With cognitive behavioral therapy it's not just one thing that makes this. There are many different things that it can help with in the mental illness field or in the medical field and being able to understand all the different components of this type of therapy is going to be able to help you go into it with your eyes open. It will also help your heart stay open as well. When you go into this trying your best it is going to give you the best results possible.

Congratulations on completing this journey to discover and enhance your leadership skills.

By reading this book you have begun to understand how emotional intelligence is fundamental to attract people, developing favorable relationships with them and profitably involve them in your projects.

The basic principles you have learned in this book will help you to enhance your communication skills to win friends, positively influence people and finally lead your team.

The next step is to start incorporating the strategies recommended in this book in your daily life and practice them consistently.

Finally, if you found this book useful, a review on Amazon is always appreciated.

As you have seen from this book, emotion regulation plays a big part in getting you to improve your emotional intelligence is by developing self-awareness and monitoring, which enables you to see how your emotions work. By exercising self-control, you can regulate your feelings constructively and healthily. You're able to get out all the negative emotions and continue to produce positive emotions, which will naturally be infectious and helpful to others. Emotions are powerful, and they influence others in many different ways, especially the "feelers" from the Myers Brigg Type Indicator. Some people feel more intensely than others.

As a manager of a company, your responsibility is to take care of your employees, and you have to be sensitive to their needs and emotional expressions. Many times, colleagues and subordinates will get frustrated and complain when times are difficult and when work is tedious and taxing. The manager needs to address the needs of his or her employees to make them happy because a happy employee makes a happy company. It is essential to gauge the emotional level of the employees within a company because you want to create an upbeat and enthusiastic atmosphere for your employees. They should want to go to work and not dread having a case of the Mondays. You want to make work exciting, enjoyable, and profitable for your workers because then they can produce the best products for your company.

We have been able to walk you through a four-week plan of monitoring of emotions within your company. We hope you have taken careful notes in the journal and notes pages that we have created for you. Emotional control and regulation will enable you to understand people within your company and their unique personalities. It gives you a taste of how to relate to others and practice intuitive social skills. Therefore, having high emotional intelligence (EQ) will allow you to make good relationships with others in ways that you didn't before. It is important to develop people skills for any vocation or job but especially for the role of the manager in a company. You have to learn how to relate to all of your employees and treat them with respect and care. Being sensitive to their emotions will give you a quality of compassion that they can identify. Moreover, the employees will respect you more if you connect with them on a relational and emotional level.

With your knowledge of emotional intelligence, we hope you can take this information and form the best relationships with your colleagues, clients, and employees. You will receive high ratings from all the people you work with and be truly successful in achieving great things if you are more emotionally sensitive. We can guarantee that people will like you more and will respect you for what you're able to see in them, a person who is worthy of honor and respect. Finally, you can achieve whatever you set out to do because when you are people-centered and oriented around others, you will find complete happiness, joy, and satisfaction in your job and company.